Lost Child Found

Trucks, Cars, and Finding Family
(Follow the DNA)

By
Paul Sperry

Copyright © 2023

by Paul Sperry

Independently Published Printed by Kindle Direct Publishing a division of Amazon.com, Inc. www.kdp.amazon.com.

All rights reserved. No part of this publication may be reproduced, stored in a retrieval system, or transmitted, in any form or by any means, electronic, mechanical, photocopying, recording, or otherwise, without the prior written permission of the author.

ISBN-13: 9798860702820

Dedication

This book is dedicated to
Virginia Evelyn Wheeler and Elliot Bennett,
the two people who created me.
I wouldn't be here if not for them.
And, of course, my adopted parents:
Ruth Hopkins Sperry and Max Willard Sperry.

Many thanks to Janet Gregory, an accomplished author and friend, for her careful editing and many helpful suggestions along the way. She motivated me at times when I needed motivation.

Many thanks Richard Dentino, Bert Howard, along with others who have read my writings and approved of them while making helpful suggestions along the way. All have been supporting me and prompting me to go further.

The Tree – Courtesy of Freepik.com

Lost Child Found

Contents

Preface 1

Section One: Living in America 1935-2005 3

Part 1: 1935, Growing up During the Depression 4
Part 2: 1945, A Big Change 20
Part 3: 1947, The Driving Years 47
Part 4: 1953, After High School 56
Part 5: 1958, Beating the Draft 71
Part 6: 1962, The Gold'n Rich Years 84
Part 7: 1978, The Busy Years 89

Section Two: Finding My Roots and Much More 109

Part 1: 2005, Following the Paper Trail 110
Part 2: 2011, Follow the DNA 115
Part 3: 2018, The Payoff 121

Epilogue 143

Family Trees 147
Questions to Ponder 149
Acronym Decoder 150

Market Street, looking toward the Ferry Building in San Francisco, c.1935 – Courtesy of Sfgate.com and the Chronical Archives

Preface

This is a true story about being born in the Great Depression, being raised during World War Two, being told at the age of twelve that I was adopted, being told I was half Czechoslovakian, all of which served me well as it turned out, and, finally much later in life when Genealogy was in full swing, a search for my ancestry began.

In the middle of the Great Depression there was terrible unemployment and the government started the C.C.C. (Civilian Conservation Corps) and W.P.A. (Works Progress Administration), but not everybody could do that. Men traveled the country hitching rides on freight trains looking for work. There were bread lines where unemployed men would stand in line for hours to get a cup of soup and a piece of bread. People used any skills they had, trying to get by until steady work became available, which didn't happen until the United States was forced into war after the Japanese attack on Pearl Harbor on December 7, 1941.

During World War Two there was plenty of work for those not actively in the military. The bread lines went away and the economy boomed due to the war effort. There were shortages though, as everything was concentrated on the defense of the country. Gas was the most noticed shortage because it was rationed; when your share was gone you couldn't drive anymore until the next ration book came out.

Lost Child Found

When I was told my birth father was Czech, I believed it until I found out in my eighties it wasn't true. During my time in the military, not knowing might have saved my life. I was busted out of a program that was rated Top Secret because I stated I was half Czech. Czechoslovakia was behind the "Iron Curtain", under the control of Russia.

Paul Sperry

San Francisco Ferry Building from above Market Street, 1928 – Courtesy of SMTA.org

Lost Child Found

Section One:

Living in America

1935-2005

Lost Child Found

Part 1: 1935, Growing up During the Depression and WW2

In San Francisco in 1935 if you wanted to get from San Francisco to Oakland or Marin County, to the north, you took the ferry across San Francisco Bay. The San Francisco-Oakland Bay Bridge, to the east, and the Golden Gate Bridge, north to Marin County, were both under construction. Market Street in San Francisco had four lines of trollies ending at the Ferry Building, where you could walk on or drive on to a ferry. There were rail connections on the Oakland side. They also had barges transporting railroad freight cars across the bay.

Ferry Boat Oakland – Courtesy of LocalWiki.org/Oakland

The San Francisco-Oakland Bay Bridge was built when I was about one year old. There was still a car ferry that went between San Francisco and Oakland, as there had been for years. I can remember being in the car when we drove out onto the 7th Street Pier in Oakland and driving onto the ferry. The pier went into the bay for a good quarter mile, apparently into deep enough water for the ferry. I don't know why we did that because it was much faster to go on the bridge. The ferry was more fun though. Once you were on, you could go up on deck and see the sights of San Francisco Bay. They also had a coffee shop with donuts where you could sit on a wooden bench and watch other boats go by. Ferries came from Marin County and other places around the bay, most going to San Francisco. The San Francisco-Oakland Bay Bridge and the Golden Gate Bridge were finished about the same time. Both bridges saved motorists hours of driving time. The Bay Bridge started in Oakland, connected to Yerba Buena Island in the middle of the bay before continuing on to San Francisco. The island was enlarged with land fill to create Treasure Island. In 1939, the World's Fair was presented there. All I can remember, at age four, was a huge motion picture screen that regularly showed two steam locomotives running head-on into each other with disastrous results.

San Francisco Bay Bridge, 1935 – Courtesy of FoundSF.org

Lost Child Found

If you drove through Golden Gate Park in the middle of San Francisco the road ended at Ocean Beach Drive, which was part of California Route One along the coast with the Pacific Ocean far below. At Ocean Beach it was flat and if you turned north there was a huge building called "The Fun House". For very little money you entered a world of slides, games, and many fun things to play with. To enter, you went through a path of mirrors that was always a challenge. In front was a huge moving statue of a laughing woman, with sound. This was always a fun destination.

Sutro Baths were nearby, if you liked Public Swimming Pools.

The Great Depression started in 1929 when the Stock Market crashed. The Dust Bowl started in 1931 with drought in Oklahoma forcing people to move because they couldn't farm anymore. This lasted until 1941 when we went to war with Japan, after they bombed Pearl Harbor.

In 1941, World War Two started for America, as the Japanese bombed Pearl Harbor. From then on and for four more years the population changed and suddenly there were jobs for everybody. The younger men went off to war and the rest were pressed into defense work. We also suddenly had rationing of food and especially gasoline.

My Uncle John and cousin Sam went off to war. John went to Florida to run a Link Trainer for pilots in the Army Air Corp. Sam was in the Army Signal Corps when they landed on the beach in Italy. He could never talk about what he did. It was all classified and he didn't want to talk about it anyway. He learned photography while in the Signal Corps, so I imagined he took pictures of enemy installations. I might have been right. Decades after the war Sam still never said a word. John suddenly was a flyer in the war if you believed his story.

Lost Child Found

On a cold foggy afternoon in San Francisco a child was born. That child was me. I was born at Saint Joseph's Hospital, high on a hill overlooking Market Street. It was the middle of the great depression and times were tough. I was placed in a "Native Daughters of the Golden West Shelter for Homeless Children". How's that for a catchy title. Kind of grabs you where you don't want to be grabbed. They had several "cottages" in the Avenues in residential San Francisco. They would place thirteen babies with a nurse in each house until they were adopted. It's a wonder I'm not still there. They fed all of us cow's milk and I for one reacted with congestion, hives, and difficulty breathing. They say I cried a lot. I probably kept everyone up at night.

Saint Joseph's Hospital (1928-1979). Now it is a Condo. – Courtesy of Wikipedia.org

Eighty-two years later I found out why I was placed in the home. My birth-mother and father had wanted to marry, but my birth-mother's mother insisted she give me away and continue to go to Stanford University to become a doctor. She had the grades, was smart, and her mother was completely overbearing. Later in my birth mother's life I was referred to as "the lost child".

At four months I was adopted by a couple that bought into a lawyer's group that would find you a baby, even if you really weren't eligible. My adopted folks lived in a converted coal bin in the basement of an apartment house in Oakland. Leaving the "cottage" had to be a positive move. Things could only get better. And they did. The first thing my folks did was move to a place that would accommodate a goat and raised me on its milk. I immediately lost my hives. The house was in the Meekland district of Hayward which was semi-rural at that time. It was on a dead-end street with a creek at the end. It was full of frogs and pollywogs in the spring. I would gather the pollywogs and bring them home in a mason jar. At the corner was a house with a magic front yard. It was full of little houses and people about four inches tall. The houses were made of some kind of stucco with tiny cedar shakes on the roof and the figures were carved from wood and painted. It had streets and sidewalks and stop signs and was in great detail. This was all done apparently by the homeowner. I remember spending a lot of time hanging on the fence taking in every detail. Along with the goat there were chickens and a mean rooster. He attacked me one day and pecked near my eye. We had him for dinner that night.

My adopted dad, Max Willard Sperry, was a farmer at heart, and he must have enjoyed Hayward. He tried growing corn, but it turned out to be "field" corn, something you would feed the cows. He loved having a vegetable garden and barnyard animals. He was born in Anaconda, Montana and grew up in McCall, Idaho. At age sixteen he ran a four-horse freight wagon around McCall. I think he and his folks must have frozen every winter in their dirt-floored log house, because they moved to Gridley, California where it gets very hot in the summer and not very cold in the winter.

My adopted mom, Ruth Ester Hopkins Sperry, was born in Nebraska and was the first of her family to move to California, in her twenties. They all seemed to move to Lodi from Nebraska. Even much older people. The word got around. If you moved to California from Nebraska, you went to Lodi. Mom went to college around there and was always interested in the English language. My dad, by contrast, thought an eighth-grade education was enough. He did take a business course at Laney Trade, in Oakland, California, much later in life which served him well.

Ruth and Max, adopted mom and dad – Sperry Family Collection

From my mom, I learned to pronounce wash as "warsh". "Go warsh your hands." I guess it's a Nebraska thing. My wife, Jane, pointed this out to me. I never realized how I pronounced it before. My mom also used to call everybody "Honey". "Your pants are on fire, honey." "Honey, please take the trash out." I don't know where that came from. I did not pick that up.

My adopted folks were loving people who gave me plenty of love, if not much else. They moved a lot. Looking back, I figured my dad would find an apartment house that was run down and fix it up for a little pay and a place to live. By the time I joined the Air Force at age 23, we had moved 27 times. The Air Force wanted to know because they wanted to put me in a Russian language program that required a very high security clearance.

When I was young, I was healthy, except for allergies to just about everything that caused me to have a runny nose. As I grew, I became a tall skinny guy who never weighed more than 130 pounds until my early twenties when I got a job in a dairy and put on thirty-five pounds of muscle in a short time. It was like lifting weights for a living and I thrived on it.

Eventually I could tolerate cow's milk and the goat was gone.

Milk could be delivered to your house, always in returnable heavy glass bottles. It would be left on your front porch early in the morning. Some houses had little doors in the side, just big enough for milk bottles. You would put the empties out the night before with a note saying how much you needed. Some places even had produce for sale off a flatbed truck and others had bread and eggs. If you had an ice box, instead of the new-fangled electric "fridge", the ice man would bring in a big chunk of ice and put it right in the ice box.

We then moved back to Oakland on Croxston Avenue near the Piedmont Avenue district. When the war started in 1941, we had air raid sirens go off at night and we would cut out all the lights. No enemy planes ever came by, but we were prepared if they did. My dad, being a Block Warden, would go out to check if lights were still on. One night we were sitting in the dark trying to figure out what was glowing in the corner. When the "All Clear" sounded, we discovered my Captain Midnight glow in the dark belt. It was probably somewhat radioactive, but who knew.

After a while we found a nearby house with a bigger yard and no neighbors upstairs. I was elected to guide the moving van driver to the new place, which was only four blocks away on Warren Avenue. Being only seven, I didn't know quite when to signal a turn. I was a little late telling the driver, but he turned anyway and ran up a telephone pole guy wire. It wasn't serious but it could have been. In the new place, my dad raised rabbits and had a real garden with real corn. We would have people over and serve rabbit and tell them it was chicken; no one could tell the difference. One couple wondered at seeing four legs but never caught on.

There was another creek across the street and I spent many hours investigating it. The water flowed out of a six-foot-high concrete pipe and eventually into Lake Merritt and the San Francisco Bay. I would walk into the tunnel with a candle as far as I would dare to go. Of course, this wonderful creek was a storm drain for that part of Oakland but the vegetation didn't care and neither did I. The street ran around the creek for several blocks and is called Richmond Blvd. It was one way on each side. It was a wonderful little jungle in the middle of a huge city.

Up a long flight of stairs was Kempton Avenue where my Grandma Lida had a boarding house. The house was built with 100% redwood, with shingles on the side. The street only went for a short block with most houses being two stories with a full basement and an attic. She occasionally had soldiers and sailors on leave visiting her. One was my cousin Sam who was in the Army Signal Corps when they invaded Italy. My Uncle John came by too. He was in the Army Air Corps and ran a Link Trainer in Tampa, Florida to teach pilots to fly. By the time he retired to Rossmoor in Walnut Creek, he claimed he was a B-25 pilot. It wasn't true sounded sexier to the ladies.

Every Saturday we would go to Oakland's Tenth Street market to shop. It was a warehouse type building with many stalls with vendors selling anything from batteries to bananas. I remember a vendor selling nothing except peas. She was a large Italian lady and she would hawk her wares by saying: "Nice-a-peasies, get your nice-apeasies", in a loud voice. A lot of it was produce, fresh off the farm.

There also was Andrew Williams grocery store, on McArthur Blvd (named after General Douglas McArthur) near Piedmont Avenue. They had an automatic doughnut maker that was fun to watch. The dough would come out of a dispenser into boiling hot oil. Something would keep it moving until another gadget turned them over. Eventually they would come up a conveyer belt onto a screen to cool. All this behind glass so you could watch the process. Nothing tasted better than a doughnut fresh off the machine.

They also had a regular bakery. I remember buying a loaf of white bread, unsliced of course, and eating some on my way home. You could just tear a hunk off the loaf and eat it. It was best warm just out of the oven.

I went to Edison Elementary school on Kempton Avenue in Oakland. It was close to my Grandma Lida's house and close enough to our house on Croxston and Warren. Folks didn't drive their kids to school then. Our graduating class consisted of three girls and two boys. Classes were so small they would teach two grades in the same room. I was put in charge of the crossing guard patrol, mainly because the only other boy in our class wrote his initials on the side of the school. No one else in school was M.M. (Mike McCann). We would march down to Harrison Street at the proper time and when students appeared, I would blow the whistle and Mike would put out the stop sign on a stick and we hoped people would stop. We would eventually march back to school.

Every school room had a "blackboard". It was a black piece of slate, hanging on the wall. You could write on it with white chalk and when you were through you would erase the chalk using an eraser. Each day someone would have to clean the erasers. It was a messy job that no one wanted, so usually someone who did something wrong would end up with that job. You cleaned them by banging two of them together until the chalk was banged out of them. Dust would fly everywhere and whoever had the job of cleaning them would have chalk dust all over them.

I lived up in the attic at Grandma Lida's house for a while. There was a tiny window in the attic that looked out over the roof at the Oakland skyline with the Oakland Tribune Tower front and center. I don't know where my folks were then. My adopted-mother would sometimes get migraine headaches. Maybe she was in the hospital.

There was a house next door that had a full basement. One day I noticed windows at ground level and heard a model train whistle. I investigated and discovered the man had a train layout filling the basement. I would lie on the grass looking in the window watching trains going by.

They were the same size as my Lionel, but much more detailed and the layout had buildings and trees with roads and cars. I thought that was the coolest thing yet.

When we moved again, it was to 1272 Pearson Avenue in San Leandro, into a new housing tract built for all the workers finding work for the war effort. By that time, my dad worked in the Kaiser Shipyards in Oakland. He was a quartermaster, whatever that is. It was the first and only house my parents owned, along with the bank of course. We had a brand new 1941 Hudson and things were looking up. I was old enough to be out of a car seat (not invented yet) and discovered I could lie in the rear window shelf. My own kids got the first car seats and they were held onto the seat by the weight of the child. They had a steering wheel to play with that probably was lethal if you crashed.

The Hudson had "suicide" rear doors. The doors were hinged at the rear. I promptly tried out the door handle as we were driving slowly down the street. The door immediately opened and both my parents were afraid I would fall out. Seat belts weren't invented yet. They were able to stop and close the door with no problems, but I learned my lesson on "suicide doors".

Dad bought a used Ford Model A pickup truck to get a better gas ration card. During the war a lot of stuff was rationed, among them gasoline. A commercial license plate got you more gas. He built a garage and shop and parked the truck in it. I was always aware of cars and trucks and saw how my dad started the Ford. It had a starter button on the floor behind and to the right of the gas pedal. One day I attempted to start it, not knowing it was in gear. As I stepped on the starter button the truck lurched forward and, luckily, I got my foot off the starter. I never did tell him about that. He had a long copper pipe, bought to make a new fuel line for the truck, I was discovering tools and decided that the pipe should be hammered flat. He was not too happy about that.

Dad had a radio that was a major piece of furniture. It sat on the floor and was about four feet high and three feet wide. It had about six bands you could dial up. Written on them were foreign city names like London, Paris, and more. There was no FM. It hadn't been invented yet. All we were ever able to dial in were KGO and KFRC and a couple more that were out of San Francisco. One day I found a tool and carved my initials in the radio. It seemed like a good idea at the time but was not appreciated. We would all gather in front of it at six o'clock and listen to Gabriel Heatter and the News. I liked "Captain Midnight" and "Jack Armstrong", the all-American boy. I would not listen to "Red Skelton" though. I thought it was "red skeleton" and that sounded too scary. One of the cowboy shows offered a square inch of West Texas if you sent in a box top from a certain cereal. I did that and received what looked like a legitimate "Deed" to acreage in West Texas. If you've ever been in West Texas, you can understand why they might want to give it away.

We didn't watch Television. It wouldn't be invented for another decade or so, and then it was black and white with just a test pattern on at times. You had to constantly adjust the vertical and horizontal dials to get a decent picture. The vacuum tubes would burn out regularly and there were test machines in every grocery store to test the tubes and sell you a new one. There were dozens of companies that would send out technicians to adjust your television set. The antennas could be a problem to install. My dad had an antenna hanging upside down from a gutter for years because the reception was best with it in that exact position.

I remember my dad coming home from work in the Kaiser Shipyards where they were building "Liberty" ships as fast as they could. He would plop into his favorite chair, take his boots off, and go to sleep for half an hour. Our brand-new house had two or three bedrooms and one bathroom. They built a bunch of them all at once in a "subdivision". You opened the door directly into the living room. When it got dark, you turned on the light in the room you were in. When you left that room, you turned the light off. It became a habit for that generation. There was no garage until my dad built one. Cars had "running boards" and kids would stand on them holding on through the open windows to get a short ride somewhere. You could also ride in the back of a pickup. Seat belts hadn't been invented yet and safety wasn't practiced then. Dad sometimes got a ride to work with a fellow that had a big Buick. He would slow down enough for Dad to run and jump on the running board. This was all to try to save gas.

Because Dad worked for Kaiser Shipyards, we were among the first people to enroll in Kaiser Permanente hospital. My number started with 01131--. I never found anyone with a lower number. I got the first experimental allergy pills there. They tested a bunch of us with free antihistamine pills. About this time, they were working on vaccines for chicken pox, measles, and polio. I got chicken pox and measles anyway. Thankfully I didn't get polio.

There was no sugar available so I would use Karo Corn Syrup on my dry cereal in the morning. We all took labels off tin cans, flattened them and saved them for the war effort. We also collected dandelion seed pods. They told us they used them in Navy "Life Preservers". I doubt that but it kept us busy at the time. My mother tried to shame me into eating all my dinner by pointing out that there were starving children in China and that I shouldn't waste food. I never did figure out why my eating habits would affect that. When we went to the movies, they would have songs on the screen and a bouncing ball you were supposed to sing along with. One movie stood out and left an impression on this eight-year-old. It showed Russian peasants being attacked by German Panzer tanks and mean looking German troops. One German soldier was scalded when a very large peasant woman managed to dump a huge pot of boiling water on him. Another Russian peasant threw himself under a Panzer tank and the tank blew up. Movies at the time usually had a cartoon and some kind of news of the day. All this in glorious black and white.

My dad only gave me a spanking once with his belt and it got my attention. I had decided to see where the city bus went, didn't get back until after dark, and of course they were worried. Worry turned into punishment time when I walked in the door. I got the idea from my older cousin MaryAnne. In Sacramento we would get on the bus and eventually it would return to the same spot. It seemed like fun and didn't cost very much. The trick was to tell your parents first. I forgot that.

The San Leandro house had a large backyard. It had been an apricot orchard and every house had an apricot tree in the back. Dad grew fantastic squash. It even went in the neighbor's yard much to their delight. My mom was never interested with what my dad grew and one day proclaimed the backyard was for me to play in. I developed roads for the semi-truck and trailer my dad made for me out of wood. They went well with the building he made with "Paul's Trucking" on the front. I then put up a tent and added a wooden floor complete with a trap door into the "basement". I then dug a tunnel out about ten feet with a garbage can lid covering the escape hatch. My parents didn't catch on for a long time. Down the street on Davis they were bulldozing an area for new houses. There was also a field of rhubarb growing and they let me cut as much rhubarb as I could carry in my wagon. My mom was surprised when I came home with a wagon full of rhubarb. She canned it and we ate it for a year.

Davis Street led to the city dump where in those days they didn't bother covering it with dirt right away, so you could smell it for miles around. The Eastshore Freeway through Berkeley had the same odor problem. All the sewage from Oakland was discharged directly into the bay near the San Francisco-Oakland Bay Bridge. That freeway was never pleasant to drive on and people tended to speed. All the time we lived in San Leandro, I still went to school in Oakland. I would ride in with Mom as she went to her job at the First Christian Church on Fairmont Ave, near Broadway and 29th. This was a good idea as far as staying in the same school but didn't help me getting to know kids in the San Leandro neighborhood.

My mother insisted I wear wool dress slacks to school and they were so itchy I wore my pajamas underneath. When she finally discovered this, she relented and let me wear comfortable clothes.

They advanced me a grade in grammar school because I already knew what they were teaching. My mother was always correcting my English when I spoke and she taught me other stuff too. This was all well and good except from then on I was always the youngest and smallest in class. This was not good as I advanced to Junior High and High school. Bullies found me easy pickings.

My Grandma Lida moved in with us as she was sick with cancer. Her son, my Uncle John, gave her a new invention they called a ballpoint pen. It was thick and chrome plated and they said it would write under water. So, everyone took a turn writing underwater with it. I don't know why you would want to write underwater, but if you did, this was the pen to use. Up to this time everyone used a pen that you would fill with ink and the ink would flow down to the metal tip that was split at the end. After writing you would blot it with, what else, a blotter. In school each desk had an ink well.

It was a hole in the desk that would hold a glass cup. You would fill this with ink and dip your pen in it and it would write a few words until it ran out and you would dip it again. These ink wells became popular for boys with a girl seated in front of them. If she had a long pigtail, it could be the ideal length to dip in the ink well. This was not so popular with the girls and could get the boy in trouble pretty quickly. Later they invented pens that could store more ink later. You would dip the pen in the ink container and operate a lever that would pump enough ink into the pen to write a couple of pages.

Part 2: 1945, A Big Change

About this time the war ended, and work was scarce for dad. He worked as a mechanic at Yellow Cab at night, but he finally decided to leave. My adopted parents divorced in 1945. One day dad was there and the next day he was gone. Mom and I ended up living in the basement of the First Christian Church in Oakland, on Fairmont Avenue, where she was a secretary. I was given a not very big box to put as many toys in as I could and told to bury the rest in my "Army" hole in the back yard. I saved my Lionel Train but had to let go of the "set of doubles" truck and a greyhound bus. At first, I thought I was to blame for the divorce because my dad always was telling me not to hang by my elbows from our very upright chairs, which I just couldn't resist doing. I had a lifetime habit of clearing my throat and sniffing, a habit not alluring to him. My mom told me I was not to blame. I got over it, but still missed having him around.

My room in the basement of the church was big enough for me to have the Lionel train set up. My room was off a long hallway that disappeared into the darkness. One day I found a flashlight and investigated the hallway. At the end I found a wonderful apparatus. It was a four wheeled "wagon" you would sit on, steer with your feet and pump with your hands to make it go. It had two gears forward and a lever for a brake. I proceeded to drag it upstairs and outside. I found I could roll down the hill and get it into second gear and go pretty fast. I then went to Hagstrom's Grocery on Broadway and found a couple of big cardboard boxes and dragged them "home". Back then the stores mostly burned cardboard boxes in an incinerator after stocking shelves. Recycling wasn't in yet. I proceeded to cut the cardboard into the general shape of a very square car. It had "lights" made of tuna fish cans and a speedometer made with a bent nail. I was ready to go. This was my first "almost" car.

I had the run of the church and remember drinking grape juice out of tiny little glasses that were left over from communion on Sunday. Dr. Reager had a rug in his office, and I would go in there with a mason jar full of pennies and learn how to count, add, and subtract.

My mother was an excellent typist. With the manual typewriters, each letter was typed onto an ink ribbon and onto the paper. When the ribbon ran out you changed the ribbon. If you typed a little fast, the letters could jam at the ribbon. When electric typewriters came out my mother could type 96 words a minute and if she made a mistake she knew where it was. Then you would paint "white out" over the mistake and re type the correct version. She could take dictation using "shorthand", while Dr. Reager talked, and then type up a written version.

During this time, we were expected to go to services, and I remember a song I couldn't figure out. It was "Onward Christian Shoulders [Soldiers], marching as to war". It just didn't make sense to me. Why would shoulders be marching?

My dad made a lighted case with a glass door to display Mom's Nativity Scene. The figures were finely made in Germany before the war and my dad built a stable inside the display case. The floor was covered in sand which made the figures more lifelike. In the back was a blue painted piece of glass with stars scratched into it with one large star in the center. This was lighted from the rear. We would set it up in the entry of the church every Christmas. On the bottom of each figure, it said "Made in Germany".

Mom's Nativity Scene 1950 – Sperry Family Collection

After World War Two, anything from Germany was marked "Made in West Germany" as the Russians occupied East Germany. Now we're back to just "Made in Germany".

One of my friends there was Leland Shoptaugh; his father ran the "Piedmont Press". He had a weekly paper and I remember watching him set type by hand in the press. He had to read the words in a mirror image and place each letter by hand in the flat press. Ink was applied and a piece of paper pressed on it one at a time. That's why they call it a "Printing Press". After running the edition, he would take it all apart and return each letter to its storage place to be ready to be used in the next edition. His hands were permanently stained with printer's ink. The other way to print a smaller edition of something was to use a mimeograph machine, which is what my mother used to print weekly Church Bulletins. That involved a barrel shaped thing with a special covering you would prepare by typing in a message. This was filled with blue ink and rotated to print each page. Either way was extremely messy and time consuming.

Lost Child Found

We finally moved from the church basement to a real house, which we shared with an "old maid" lady who had her own room upstairs. This house on Yosemite Avenue was so old that the light in the kitchen was at the end of a tube that came down from the ceiling and curved back up. It still had a valve in it from when they had gas lights. The bulb itself was huge and had a curlicue in the top. It was there when we moved in and it was there when we moved out seven years later. It still may be there.

Black Candlestick Telephone – Courtesy of Model T Ford Forum

The telephone was upright and had a speaking tube and you lifted the earpiece to your ear to hear. The operator would say, "Number please" and you would say something like "Glencourt 2212". That was an uncle's number in case of emergency. The operator would also give you the correct time, a good thing with the wind-up alarm clocks everybody had then. Later modern phones had a dial you operated with your finger, but we still had the older style. Back then, the phone company owned the phone, so you took what they offered, and it was always black.

The doorbell was right in the middle of the front door. It had a spring on the inside and when you pushed it, it would go in and pop back out, making a ringing sound when it did. No electricity was involved.

The gas furnace was under a grate in the floor of the dining room. You lit it with a match attached to the end of a long heavy wire. After the burner lit, you adjusted it with a handle, and it ran until you shut it off. No thermostat involved. You had to avoid walking on the grate, especially when barefoot. It would get pretty hot.

The light switches in the house were two round buttons for on or off. When you pushed in one the other would pop out.

The living room was separated from the dining room by glass doors with little panes that slid into the wall to either open up and connect the two rooms or separate them. The dining room had a "window" that opened into the kitchen with a roll up door. You could slide stuff from the kitchen into the dining room and then close the little door. The dining room was completely paneled in very dark wood. The living room had windows with a bench next to them and a storage area underneath. The kitchen had a pantry with the sink at the end.

Back then when you moved you took your stove and refrigerator with you. Our refrigerator was probably all of 6 cubic feet with a "freezer" just big enough for two ice trays. You would fill the trays with water, place them on the shelves and eventually you had ice. The stove would have to be hooked up to the stove pipe and also the gas bib. Electric stoves weren't used very much. The water heaters were usually made with a copper tank and would last for 50 years. The sewer pipes were made of cast iron and were sometimes attached on the outside of the house. I guess this was the easiest way to do it if you were converting to inside plumbing.

The house had an enclosed back porch where there were laundry tubs. You hooked up your wringer washing machine and filled it with water from the faucet over the laundry tubs. You could save rinse water and use it again by pumping it back into the washer. Nothing on it was automatic. When you were through washing and rinsing you ran the clothes through a "wringer" that squeezed some of the water out, and then you hung them to dry in the sun on a clothesline with clothes pins. The pins came in several styles, some with springs but all made from wood. Then you ironed your clothes with an iron you heated on the stove or used the newer electric iron that just plugged into the wall. There were no wrinkle free clothes at that time. People even ironed their sheets, some on a big roller machine that ironed more surface at a time.

We lived off Piedmont Avenue again and Piedmont Avenue had an electric streetcar that ran all the way from the cemetery at the end of Piedmont Avenue to Jack London Square in downtown Oakland. We would put pennies on the track and retrieve them flattened, after the streetcar went by. Up Piedmont Avenue to 41st there was a Station for the electric Key System Train that went to San Francisco. This was a two-, four- or six-unit electric train that ran across the San Francisco Bay Bridge on the lower deck next to the two-way truck lanes, with a "suicide" lane in the middle, meant for passing. That middle lane caused a lot of accidents. If you were lucky, you could sit in the front row seat and look straight ahead at the tracks, watching for trains going the other way, and watch the truck traffic over in their lanes. The operator sat on the right side of the train in his own little compartment. The upper deck of the bridge was for two-way automobile traffic.

When they decided to switch to diesel buses, they decided to pull the rails out of the streets. I watched how they did it on Piedmont Avenue. They had a big truck with a boom on the back. They would run a steel cable up the boom and down to the track and attach it to the track. Then they would reel in the cable, like a tow truck, to pull up the track. That was the plan. When they tried, the track wouldn't come up. They proceeded to plan B. They would reel in the cable which would cause the front of the truck to go up in the air quite a ways. They would then release the tension on the cable until the truck almost hit the ground, and then reapply tension on the cable. This would cause the truck to stop in midair and hopefully the train rail would be pulled up a little. It was a slow process, but it worked. I was amazed the truck, and especially the driver, could take all that bouncing around.

On 40th Street, off Piedmont Avenue, there was a "Fixit Shop". If you brought your broken toaster or coffee pot to "Mr. Fixit" he could get it going again for a lot less money than a new one. Try doing that today.

Good luck.

They came out with a new product called Oleo Margarine. It was a cheaper substitute for butter. It was white but was in a plastic bag with a color button you could smash and then work the color into the margarine while it was still contained in the plastic bag, then it looked more like butter. The butter lobby wouldn't allow it to be sold with the color already mixed in. When you were through mixing the color around, you had to somehow get it out of the bag. Now you had a one-pound piece of stuff you had to get cold and cut into at least quarter-pound blocks to be usable. The whole thing was a chore nobody looked forward to doing.

About six blocks up Piedmont Avenue was the Piedmont Theater. Occasionally I would go to the movies. One night, walking home by myself, a drunk man came stumbling out of the Piedmont Bar and startled me. I could smell his foul breath and I ran the six blocks home. This was my first encounter with a drunk. My folks never drank anything stronger than coffee and not much of that.

Once, I came across a man walking down Piedmont Avenue who had the biggest muscles I had ever seen. He was so overly built he scared me. He looked like he could pick up a train. I saw him again and discovered he ran a shop on Piedmont Avenue. He sold weights and exercise equipment and taught classes. His name was Jack Dillinger, no relation to the gangster John Dillinger. Forty years later I saw him walking down College Avenue in Oakland. He still walked everywhere and still had big muscles and still had a weight shop. He was very friendly, and we talked a while.

My grandfather, on my mother's side, died in Sacramento, so we took off from Oakland on the river road to go to his funeral. There was no Highway 80 freeway at that time. North of Antioch, there were farmers plowing fields. One of them pulled onto the highway with his tractor and left great globs of mud on the already wet road. My mother didn't have a chance. She started to slide, and I remember looking out the side window at the fields and wondering how the road suddenly came into view. Next thing I knew, I was sitting on the rear window of the Hudson with all our luggage piled on top of me. Mom cried out, "Are you OK?" I said "Yes. How are you?" We were unhurt, but the car was upside down in a ditch with the top crushed in, along with the four fenders, hood, and trunk. People helped get it upright on the road again and towed us to a gas station. No glass was broken, and the doors still operated. We filled up all the liquid levels, kicked the top up to where we could see out and continued on our journey. Then back to Oakland, the body shop actually beat the car back into shape and we drove it another eight years.

Every summer My mom would go camping with me for two weeks until I was 16. Then she would go by herself. She bought a one-wheel trailer as she could not figure out how to back up a car, let alone one with a trailer. We would load up everything including the kitchen sink and a homemade privy. Early in the morning we would take off from Oakland and eat breakfast in Tracy. The idea was to get through the valley before the heat. I always enjoyed traveling. I was always interested in other vehicles, what was happening on the road, what traffic was doing, and how other drivers were driving. My cousin MaryAnn would read a book or go to sleep. Not me. Mom always went to the same place, up Sonora Pass to Clark Fork of the North Fork of the Stanislaus River and almost to the end of the road. We carried a canvas bag full of water, hanging in front of the grill. The idea was the mist coming off the bag full of water would help cool the radiator. It would finally overheat in the mountains anyway and then we would rest for 15 minutes and add water to the radiator from the bag of water. When we got to our favorite spot, I would fill in the ditch, and we would drive the Hudson into the woods out of sight of the road and set up camp. I would dig out the ditch and no one would know we were in there. It was from here that I hiked up to Twin Lakes one day. It turned out to be a very long hike (ten miles) and I didn't get back until after dark. I ended up running down the trail, trying to beat the darkness. I ran full speed into the barbed wire gate that I had forgotten about. I ended up struggling into camp bloody and dirty and very late. Mom was so relieved to see me, I was able to talk her into letting me drive the Hudson up to Kennedy Meadow the next day. Of course, I took side trips on the way and managed to lock myself out of the car on the way. Cars had "wing" windows especially in the front doors. They could be opened and direct air at your face or just for some ventilation. Handy, as there was no air conditioning at that time. I forced a wing window to get back in and never told Mom. I was all of 12 years old at the time. The Hudson was a very well-built car, but absent any luxury. It didn't even have a heater or radio, let alone electric windows or door locks. Everything was manual and lasted forever.

I started spending part of summer wherever dad was, and always felt bad when returning to Oakland because I enjoyed myself so much. On the second trip up north to live with Dad, he was at a ranch owned by several Native American brothers he had met in the shipyard. They and their wives and kids all lived in a big house with a huge room where the kitchen and living room all ran together. Family rooms weren't invented yet. There were at least seven bedrooms off the main room.

Dad and I were in a travel trailer parked by the irrigation ditch.

We would all eat together around a really long table. We always had whatever they grew there, including big bowls of chicken, beef and pork, and more vegetables than I had ever seen. These were passed around the table and if you were lucky, some was left by the time it got to you. There was always more, back in the kitchen.

They also grew wheat and had a combine they would take around the country to other people's fields. That summer I "sewed sacks" on it all summer in the Redding area heat. The harvested grain came down a chute and was diverted into one of two receivers that you attached a sack onto. When a sack was full you could divert the grain flow into the other sack. That gave you time to sew up the top of the sack with a big needle and thread and then push the sack off the machine onto the ground. When you hung another sack, on the receiver, you were ready to do the whole thing all over again.

The two brothers, driving the tractor and combine, would wear long underwear and drink beer all day to combat the heat. I wore a hat. The trick with sewing sacks on a wheat combine was to push the full sack off without falling off yourself, more learning about leverage.

I was popular there with the wives as I would get all the younger kids together and we would do projects like pan for gold in Cow Creek and even run a sluice box. We moved a lot of gravel, but I don't think there ever was any gold in Cow Creek.

They had an outhouse, equipped with a Sears catalog, and everyone always seemed to have a bar of soap when they went swimming in Cow Creek.

They had two huge draft horses that they would hitch to a wagon and gather hay with. It was my job to guide the horses, as if I could control them. I had one shift his weight and a hoof ended up on my foot, and I was anchored to the ground until he shifted his weight again. Luckily, we were in plowed soil.

I helped a plumber one time, and he asked me to move my end of a pipe to the west. This to a city kid that measured in city blocks and uptown or downtown. That was my first awareness of direction by the compass. After that, I became more aware of where the sun was during the day and what that meant, a new concept.

After the men returned from work, we would go to a swimming hole on Cow Creek. All the kids would sit on the back of a flatbed pickup truck, with our legs hanging over the edge. We would drive down an old dirt road at slow speed because it was so rough. Occasionally one of us would be bumped off if we hit a bump. You had to scramble and run to get back on, usually while it was still moving. There was always a bar of soap to be passed around, while we swam and played in the water. If you were real daring, you could climb up on the bridge and jump off into the water. There was a rope hanging from a tree that branched out over the water. I could swing off of that. After that we would all go back and sit around that long-long table for dinner. There was no TV to watch, no cellphone to entertain you, and we didn't miss them a bit. We entertained ourselves.

Another time, Dad had me selling vegetables door-to-door out of the Gridley area. The boss had a pickup full of produce and we had buckets. The other kid told me a scam he used to sell more. He would look at the name on the mailbox and ask if Mrs. Whatever was home. If she was, he would try to sell something. If she wasn't, he would say she asked him to bring by ten pounds of potatoes or something. He got away with it but I knew that was wrong so I never tried it. I remember going to sleep on the way home in the back of the pickup, sleeping on sacks of potatoes. You have to be pretty tired to do that.

My dad's mother was still around then, and I would mow her lawn for her. She would always come out and complain about all the noise I was making with the electric lawn mower. I never did understand that. She would also unplug the electric clock when she left the house to save electricity. One day Dad had me help him load hay bales into the Model A pickup. It was hot in Gridley, and I started to sweat. I had never sweat before and asked what this moisture was. He laughed and pronounced me a man.

I usually traveled north, on the bus, to spend part of the summer with dad. This time it was winter, and I took the train. I was twelve and again traveling alone. It was no big deal back then. I somehow got down to the 16th Street Station in Oakland and got on a big green Pullman Car with hard wooden seats. The locomotive was steam, diesels weren't out yet. I enjoyed the sound of the steam, the smoke, the whole experience, especially starting to pull the heavy cars. They would sometimes spin the drive wheels with an exotic "chug-chug-chug" sound. Sometimes, they would back up a little to get started. This would cause a lot of noise as each car backed into the next one. This released tension on all the couplers so the engine would start pulling one car, and then the next, and then another as the couplers took up the slack. It was a fine art to get going without spinning the wheels. The train finally pulled into Redding, after dark on a cold winter night, after stopping at every town along the way. I picked up my one suitcase and wandered into the station to find Dad. He wasn't there. I looked everywhere. What could have happened to him? Did he forget I was coming? Did I get there a day early or late? Maybe he went off the road on the way to pick me up. It was late in the year and I knew the roads were slick with rain and snow. I knew he was living up in the mountains at the time. All these thoughts went through my mind as I patiently waited. I decided to wait an hour, then another before I would alert someone to my situation. Finally, he came in the door. His shirt was sprinkled with blood. I was very concerned. "What happened?" I exclaimed. "Shush" he said. "I'll tell you later." So, I "shushed". We went out into the rain and got in his trusty Model A pickup. He always carried his Winchester 30-30 carbine in the truck, usually in the bed or under the seat. He treated it like an old hammer, just a tool. A tool he was expert in using. He never aimed with the iron sights, he just pointed. This time the gun was propped against the seat. Finally, he told me why he was late. On his way down the mountain, he spotted a deer. It wasn't legal at that time of the year, but he was living off the land and was hungry. He stopped, grabbed the 30-30 and pointed it at the deer and fired. The deer ran off so Dad followed. After about 100 feet he saw his prey and fired again. This time it went down. He approached the animal and discovered he brought down two deer. Now he had two deer to take back home and skin and dress before he came for me. First things first. It took him a while.

On the way up the mountain, it started to snow. I was overjoyed. "Oh boy, snow," I shouted. "Oh nuts, snow," my dad replied. He proceeded to put chains on the Model A pickup for the rest of the journey.

He was living in an old one-room log-type cabin with his old travel trailer pulled up next to it. He built a hallway in between to connect them and hung coats on the wall in the hallway. He said, "Look at this" and opened the "wall" like a door. The space between the cabin and the trailer was an open air "room" where he hung deer and any other game he could find. It was cold enough out that it worked fine as an open-air refrigerator.

We ate venison and sourdough biscuits the whole time I was there. He also had a cow for milk, chickens for eggs, and an occasional fryer. He also had a horse. He was living like the mountain man he was.

He was living there while he placed a concrete foundation under a 100-year-old barn that was built with wooden pegs and square nails. He had returned to his favorite way of making a living. He was a master carpenter who could start with the foundation, build the structure and then build the cabinets and put a roof on the place. I was never able to pound a nail in a board without splitting the wood and bending the nail. Much of what I did build was held together with nuts and bolts through drilled holes.

There was a couple with three kids, living nearby, in a trailer. They all shared the cow's milk and the chickens' eggs and also the sourdough starter. Dad knew the man from working in the shipyards. The man would later become my stepbrother when dad married "Rocky's" mother. While I was there, I played with the older boys. All the kids had orange faces. Rocky found a crate of oranges and they discovered you could eat too many oranges and turn orange. Rocky got his nick name in the shipyards. Everybody wanted to know where the others were from and what the soil was like there. Lemiel was from Arkansas, where the soil was rocky, so he became "Rocky", an instant nickname, that stuck.

Dad married a woman who had a daughter and four boys. I was a little older than the youngest. We would hunt together and they loved to have me along because I would see deer before they did. When I later joined the Air Force, I found out why. I'm color blind and see shapes better, even when surrounding vegetation is the same color as the prey.

I used to do jigsaw puzzles upside down as I put them together by shape, not by color.

On one of our first outings, my stepbrothers handed me a 10-gauge shotgun to shoot. I had never shot a gun before, and they didn't warn me of the kick I was about to get. When I landed flat on my back after shooting, they all praised me for not dropping the gun, in between their laughter. They were always testing "the city boy" even when I was much older. They brought me along on an expedition to find firewood in the winter. Cedar was good because it was ready to burn immediately. We started splitting the wood with an axe and when it was my turn, everyone turned to watch "the city boy" destroy himself. I surprised them with my ability.

Dad's new wife, Laura, was from Arkansas. By the end of summer, I would have an Arkansas accent.

On one trip home on the bus, I had a venison sandwich to eat. When I got home, an FBI man soon appeared at the door asking for me. I was sure it had to do with the sandwich because the meat was probably poached out of season. I was much relieved to discover he was just looking for yet another brother, Larry, that I had never seen, who was a draft dodger. The closest I had ever been to him was a 100 feet or so. He was flying a plane and dipped his wings as he buzzed us. "There goes Larry," someone said. Laura named her children Lemiel, Larry, Lucille, Leonard, and Hubert. I don't know why Hubert.

Maybe she ran out of names beginning with "L".

All through this moving around I was kept in the same school, even when we moved to San Leandro. As a result, most of my friends were from that school. In Junior High, my best friend was Willie Ozawa. He was Japanese and we never talked about the war or internment, although looking back his family must have been interned somewhere. When we knew each other, he lived in West Oakland. I would ride my bike to his house to visit. His mother spoke no English and I spoke no Japanese, but we communicated just fine. She always insisted I bring my bike into the house. She thought it might be stolen while we visited. When graduation came, Willie went to McClymond's and I went to Tech High, where Clint Eastwood had gone a few years earlier. Willie and I never saw each other again. I guess we were both too busy just living.

While at Westlake Junior High I had a couple of run-ins with bigger kids, which was just about everybody. I was standing in a group of students waiting to go to class, when suddenly, I heard and felt someone spit on my back. With no thought at all, I spun around, and punched the person as hard as I could, which wasn't that much. About the time he went "OOF" I realized he was a dreaded Pachuco. Now they're known as Latino gang members. Bad thoughts went through my head as I looked at this kid who was a foot taller and outweighed me by 75 pounds. As I looked up at him expecting to get clobbered at any moment, he surprised me by giving me a hug and declaring to everyone in sight "This here's my buddy. Don't mess with him." He then carefully wiped the spittle off my back, and I never had another problem all through

Junior High. I don't think he had ever had anybody challenge him before, even by accident.

In music class, I sat in the next-to-the-last seat in a row. The boy behind me kept pulling my hair and generally harassing me. We were singing out of very large song books, and I had enough. He pulled my hair. So I closed the book, turned around, and hit him with the book on the side of his head as hard as I could. I turned back around and continued singing. The teacher's eyes got huge, but she never did or said a thing. The boy never touched me again.

Teachers weren't against using a wooden ruler on bare hands for punishment. I discovered this when the teacher left the room one day. I taunted the girl who was left in charge, with one of those pens you dipped in the ink well. Unfortunately, it still had a drop of ink in it, and it dripped onto the teacher's ink blotter that covered most of her desk. When she returned, I had to confess and received a couple of good whacks on the back of my hand with a wooden ruler.

Money was really scarce, so mom got me a job with the Shopping News. On Wednesday and Saturday, I would arrive back at the church from school to find a tall stack of thick papers to deliver in a certain area of Oakland. This gave me enough money that I was expected to buy some of my clothes. It was fine with me as I got to pick out what I liked. I bought shoes at J.C. Penny's because the soles were thick, and they could be re-soled three times before they wore out.

One Saturday, I left the papers on the sidewalk and went to a movie, intending to deliver them later. By the time I got back my supervisor was there and I was in trouble. I thought he would fire me, but he allowed me to deliver the papers late and I never did that again. Come to find out, some delivery boys were throwing the papers down the storm drain instead of delivering them. I guess he appreciated that I hadn't done that.

We lived in the house on Yosemite Avenue for seven years, which was half my life by the time we moved. Through all the moves, Mom managed to drag her beloved Tappan gas range and Frigidaire refrigerator with her. I managed to drag my Lionel train. We had half the downstairs and the upstairs. We shared this with Grace who used the kitchen and bath but stayed mostly in her room. The lady next door was waiting for the war to be over and her husband to get out of the Navy. She had a smart little dog that would get in the cabinet for his canned dog food and tear off the label. We all saved tin cans for the "war effort" and the dog knew about tearing off the label. They had a beautiful black 1936 three window Ford coupe. In the winter, she would drain the radiator every night and refill it with water the next morning to get to work. Anti-freeze wasn't around yet. Her husband's name was "Cupe". When he got out of the Navy, they moved to San Leandro into one of the housing tracts that were being built as fast as the builders could build them.

Mom decided we needed a couple of cats, so she acquired two mostly Persian cats. They had long black fur and were indoor-outdoor cats. Fanny got hit by a car and Felix learned from that and avoided them. He had the run of the house and neighborhood. My bedroom was upstairs and looked out over the roof. The windows swung out and Felix knew how to get on and off the roof and so used my bedroom as his room. He was not exactly a mouser. He would bring home mice for us to admire, but none were ever over an inch long. Maybe he was scared of the bigger ones. He wouldn't think of hurting them. He grew to weigh 18 pounds and some people asked, "What is he?" The long fur added about ten pounds to his appearance. When we moved seven years later we took him with us, but he kept going back to the old neighborhood which required crossing a very busy McArthur Blvd. We finally left him there as he obviously had several people feeding him.

As a turnkey kid, I needed something to do to stay out of trouble or so my mom thought. It would also get some of the housework done. So, I had a chart of chores to do every day of the week. We had a Sears upright vacuum with a big cloth bag on it. The vacuum bag would blow up like a balloon and suck in dirt and that would make your house cleaner. That was the plan. After vacuuming in front of a bright light one day, I discovered in reality it was sucking in dirt and redistributing it all over the place through the bag. That's why I always dusted after, instead of before, vacuuming. I never got paid for it. It was just a way I could help my mother keep the place up. Later I found out some kids got an allowance. I didn't know what that was. When they told me they got paid every week and they didn't have to work for it, I was amazed. I wasn't jealous though, as I made my own money and was proud of that.

I didn't know we were poor until I visited someone's house and saw what they had. It didn't matter. We didn't need much, and by then I had a job delivering real newspapers. I remember going by a gas station about this time and noticed everybody was excited and yelling. I asked why and they announced, "The war is over". I wasn't nearly as excited as they were. At ten I was the youngest delivery boy at my new job with The Oakland Tribune. Papers were about four inches wider than now, and much thicker. They were just the right length to line the garbage can. At that time there were no black plastic bags. I got to keep my own money, after buying some of my own clothes. I opened a savings account at the American Trust Bank, on Piedmont Avenue, made monthly deposits and watched my money grow.

After my first collection for the paper, I had to mail money to the Oakland Tribune office. I had never done this before and had no idea how to do it. I managed to stuff the money and coin into an envelope, put a five-cent stamp on it and dropped it into the mailbox. I was relieved when it sounded like it didn't break upon landing on the bottom. Soon a kindly mail man came to the door and explained to me that was not how you do it. From then on, I would go to a used bookstore on Piedmont Ave; that sold money orders. Every month, I would get the money order, and buy a used "Zane Grey" book. Zane Grey was a popular author of the time who wrote stories about cowboys.

I became a little hustler, finding all kinds of ways to make money, as I discovered the benefits of having some. I would pick fruit from someone's tree, with permission of course, and sell them in wax sandwich bags. I would also ask if they would like to get rid of those pesky deposit bottles everyone had. Every beverage company bottled in glass bottles, and you paid a deposit on them. You were expected to bring them back to the store to be used over and over. A much better idea than throwing away plastic, that hadn't been invented yet and ends up in the ocean. Most of the money went to my bank savings account and stayed there.

One day my mother came home from work to find her turnkey kid putting a bicycle together out of a huge box. She was amazed I was able to get money out of my bank account, ride the bus across town to Montgomery Wards, buy the bike and manage to get it back home on the bus. It was an English three-speed racer, a Raleigh, with skinny tires and a three-speed shift lever on the top cross bar. All of this without a word to her beforehand. Looking back, it's amazing to me. Times were different then. I discovered if you put a couple of playing cards near the spokes with a clothes pin they would make a noise like an engine as you pedaled. I bought a speedometer for it that went to 60 mph. Of course, I had to test it. There was a long steep hill that ended up by the Grand Lake Theater. I got going so fast that the speedometer pegged out and then broke. Luckily, I was able to stop at the bottom using the little rubber pads that squeezed on the tire rims. Actually, they worked pretty good. Kind of like disc brakes on a modern car.

Sometimes I would ride my bike to Emeryville to watch the Oakland Acorns play baseball. They let kids in free if they were accompanied by an adult. I would slip in next to a family and they never knew I was alone. There was also a Model Train Club in Emeryville that had a room full of "O" gauge trains and another with "HO" gauge trains that were half the size. You entered through an old caboose. One time I was able to bring my HO train and run it on their tracks. That was neat.

The only other boy my age on Yosemite Avenue was Ronny Hemsworth. We would play baseball in the street using a tennis ball as they didn't break windows as fast as a real baseball. One day we stepped aside for a car and it stopped. The driver asked how we were doing and introduced himself as Jacky Jensen. Apparently, he was a professional baseball player. It was lost on us as we had never heard of him. I found out later he played for the

Cleveland Indians and was a great football player in college.

Every year Ronny's grandfather, who lived with them, would have white grapes delivered in front of the house. There would be a dozen or so lugs of grapes to be carried into the basement. There was a big wooden vat that the grapes would go in and then all the kids in the neighborhood were invited to get in it and stomp the grapes. This was a yearly ritual and something different to do. By some mysterious process the smashed grapes eventually became wine for the year.

Ronny and I would play "cowboys and indians "and I decided I needed a new six-shooter. We had mail order catalogs, before the internet, and I found a replica Smith and Wesson 38 Police Special and ordered it. It looked real except for the trigger which was solid with the trigger guard. I found a file and took care of that. Now, it really looked real. It fooled the guys up at the gym on Piedmont Avenue where I sometimes hung out. One day, it disappeared. I couldn't very well ask Mom if she had seen my gun. I'm sure she had.

When I stayed with my dad, during part of the summer, I always enjoyed myself, learning and discovering things that were not available living in the big city. I watched pigs being born, cows milked, chickens laying eggs and what it takes to prepare one to eat. No meat in a plastic tray here. There was always something different to do, using your imagination or a new place to go look at.

I decided I would run away and go live with dad. I planned on fishing my way up the Sacramento River to Redding and then on to wherever he was. I packed my little canvas backpack and got my fishing pole and was ready to go. I set my Baby Ben windup alarm clock for three in the morning. When it went off, I proceeded downstairs and out the front door. That's when I discovered it was really cold out there. I changed my mind and went back to bed. I never tried again.

Across the street was a large unfinished yard that held a couple of old cars. An older boy lived next to it. There was an old Ford sedan, and he would sit in it and listen to the radio. This quickly led to a dead battery. He asked me to help him get it started to charge up the battery. The plan was for him to push the car forward and I would pop the clutch, in gear, to get it running. If it started it would crash into a wall. Therefore, the plan was for me to have it in reverse. I argued with him about that not working but he was older and insisted it would. So, he pushed the car forward and I popped the clutch with it in reverse and nothing happened. Then I realized I knew more about cars than he did.

On my paper route, I went by the Shell station on MacArthur Boulevard and Piedmont Avenue. One day I saw a car that I heard about but had never seen. It was an Aston Martin, from England, and it was towing a trailer, of all things. They were having a problem with the trailer lights. They would put a new bulb in and it would glow bright and then burn out. I watched this for a while and suggested they try a 12-volt bulb instead of the 6-volt ones they were burning up. They were desperate and so took the advice of the paperboy and tried it. Of course, it worked, and everybody was amazed the paperboy knew to do that. I knew most American cars had a six-volt electrical system, while some imports had twelve-volt systems. If you used a six-volt bulb in a twelve-volt system, the bulb would burn out. If you used a twelve-volt bulb in a six-volt system, the bulb would be dim. Why I knew this at such a young age, I have no idea, except I was always interested in anything with wheels.

About this time, I became really interested in model HO size trains. It started with my beloved Lionel. HO models were more realistic than my old Lionel and half the size and came in a box full of wood and metal parts you had to assemble with glue, paint them and put on decals. Again, plastic hadn't been invented. I decided to build a layout in the dirt side of the basement in our 100-year-old rental house. I decided I needed gravel and knew the water company was working down the street. I asked one of the men if I could have a couple of buckets of gravel, for my train. They said OK, just get it after 4:00pm. I got a bucket and a shovel and hung them on the handlebars of my trusty Wards bike and started down the street. Next thing I knew, I was rolling around on the pavement with my front teeth broken and my bike broken. So much for building a layout in the basement.

The dentist insisted he couldn't cap my teeth until I was 18. The doctor didn't catch that my broken teeth ended up in my upper lip. I went through Junior High and High School with a fat lip and broken upper teeth. The tooth pieces finally started coming out of my lip about eight years later, about the time the dentist finally installed a bridge. The dentist chair had a round porcelain bowl with a tube that ran water into it continually. Every once in a while, I could rinse out my mouth with water and spit in the bowl. I miss that feature.

The dentist's drill was run by a motor through a complicated system of cables and pulleys. He would say things like "Oops" or "Oh darn". Once he became all flustered and exclaimed "I can't work on you anymore, you're bleeding all over the place". As if it were my fault.

Lost Child Found

That was a rough couple of years for me. My folks got divorced, I broke my teeth, got stung near the eye from a bee and, while riding my bike I had a dog bite me on the leg.

I had to have a bike for my paper route. It was one of the biggest routes the Tribune had. It was so big that on Sunday morning you would find me walking noisily up Piedmont Avenue, with its trolley tracks, with two wagons in tow with wooden orange crates in them. I would fill the crates and my over-the-shoulders paper bag and rattle on my way. For the other days, I needed the bike. The bike store sold me a bunch of spokes to repair the front wheel but insisted I would never get it together, let alone balance it. They didn't know me, and my patient resolve to figure stuff out, see how they worked, and maybe fix them. The wheel was a challenge, but one of many I figured out and fixed over the years.

I finally built an HO gauge train layout on a four-foot by eight-foot table with a sheet of plywood put together by a nice carpenter neighbor. It fit right next to the dining room table. I would buy wooden track base of whatever shape I wanted and add the rails with tiny spikes. Then I had to solder the rails together as the locomotive ran on electricity through the rails. I would heat the soldering iron on Mom's gas kitchen stove and run in and solder while it was hot. Then, I would file the top smooth. I was always too busy to get in trouble.

When I was around age twelve, my mother told me about the birds and the bees. At the same time, she mentioned, "Oh, by the way, you were adopted. I'm not your 'real' mother." She also said I was half Czech. After I figured out what that meant, I thought that was cool. I didn't know anybody who was full Czech let alone half Czech. At this point, my mother explained to me that the reason I was adopted was they really wanted a baby, and this was the only way it could happen, and they really wanted me. This made me feel secure and loved. I now wondered about my birth-parents. What they looked like, what they did, where they were now. I wondered if they ever thought of me or would someday come back for me. It didn't really bother me that I was adopted. It was just another fact of life. I couldn't do anything about it, even if I wanted to. So, I didn't think about it too much.

Adoption – Courtesy of Creative Commons NounProject.org

Lost Child Found

Part 3: 1947, The Driving Years

I was 12, and a good friend of my mother's had a Chrysler car with a semi-automatic clutch that was easier to operate than "normal" cars. Amazingly, she asked If I would like to drive. She showed me how to operate everything and allowed me to drive it all over the place. It was easy to drive because you couldn't go wrong with the clutch. Once you got going, you never had to touch it again. It was as close to an automatic transmission as they had then. Later, I would borrow our trusty Hudson and "practice parking". I would move the seat all the way forward and sit on a pillow and secretly drive out to the Oakland Airport, a distance of probably 15 miles. The Hudson clutch ran in a liquid called "Hudsonite" and the transmission shifted with Hudson's hydraulic pneumatic assist. If you shifted as fast as you could it was smooth. If you shifted at a "normal" speed, it would grind the gears. I learned quickly how to "speed shift". On one of my trips, a blinking red light started up behind me. I didn't know what to do, so I slowed down to the speed limit and finally turned right onto another street, making sure to stick my arm out the window and signal. Turn signals wouldn't be around for another decade. Fortunately for me, the cop kept going.

My mother decided to drive to L.A. to see an aunt. We started out from Oakland and crossed the San Francisco - Oakland Bay Bridge. At Ocean Beach in San Francisco, we turned south on Highway One and proceeded on our way. At Ocean Beach, it was level and I talked Mom into letting me drive. She finally relented and promptly went to sleep. She awoke to find me driving along the cliffs around Devils Slide and asked how long we were on this treacherous road. I said, "a while". She said I was doing fine and went back to sleep. So, I drove Highway One to L.A. when I was 13.

My mom was the only person I knew who actually kept gloves in the glove compartment. She would start the car, reach over and get the gloves out of the glove compartment and pull them on. By this time, the car was warmed up enough to move and everyone had buckled their seat belt. Oh wait, seat belts hadn't been invented yet. The car didn't have a heater so in the winter we had small blankets to cover our legs if we got cold. It didn't have a radio either. Of course, FM stereo and tape decks and HiFi weren't around yet. If you slowed or were going to turn, you were expected to stick your arm out the window and signal which way you were going to go. Left was straight out; right was straight up and slow was wagging your hand straight down. Trucks had a similar system where a mechanical arm would do the same thing, but neither system was much good if you were in a blind spot. There were no power brakes or power steering then either. All cars had drum brakes and if they weren't kept adjusted the car would pull to one side or the other. They would also fade on a long hill. The Hudson had hydraulic brakes which were better than the older mechanical brakes. Mom had the oil changed every 1000 miles, just like everybody else. The oil was so bad back then you had to. It would drain out in a black color, but it left most of the dirt in the engine. On one occasion, the gas station neglected to put the drain plug back in. The light probably came on but nobody noticed. It actually made it almost to Sacramento, a distance of almost 100 miles, before the engine seized. Mom got a rebuilt engine out of that one.

The first grocery baskets were just a basket that you put on a folding four wheeled rack. When done, you stacked the baskets in one pile and folded the racks in another pile. My first attempt at a real job was to go to a little store down the street called Safeway. I hung around there for a week stacking baskets and collapsing racks and cleaning up anything broken and making myself useful. The clerks loved me. After a week, I asked for a paying job, and that's when they told me I would have to apply at corporate headquarters in another town. What a letdown.

Meanwhile, my broken teeth were very much alive making it hard to eat ice cream, but I managed. Even the air passing over the broken ends was painful. The dentist insisted he could do nothing until I was 18. As a result, there are very few pictures of me smiling as a teenager as it hurt too much. I also had a fat lip until years later a piece of tooth worked its way to the surface and I managed to grab it with pliers and yank it out. Eventually, my fat lip returned to normal shape.

About this time, I got my first hourly pay job. I went to work at a bakery on Piedmont Avenue when I was 13. I could walk to work, and I did. I was the general dish washer, including hundreds of cooking sheets that never seemed to run out. My first day on the job, they all stopped working and went to lunch. I thought, "Wow, what a great place to work. They let you stop to eat lunch." I started to go back to work after finishing my brown bag lunch and the boss stopped me and explained the half hour wasn't up yet. I thought I was in heaven. I get to eat and just sit around for the half hour. Only later did I discover we didn't get paid for that time. Soon, they had me assembling pies with a wringer machine. I would place the precut dough into the wringer, turn it around and once more through and you had a round piece of dough. Placed on the pan, you then put on exactly one pound of whatever fruit pie you were making and then the top crust. A round gadget then trimmed the edges, and you had a pie, ready to bake.

The bakery oven was huge with a roll up door 18 inches high and about 12 feet wide. Occasionally someone would have to get in the oven and ride the "Ferris wheel" racks around to the bottom to clean the burners and retrieve dropped pans and their contents. It never really cooled off, so that was not a pleasant thing to do. Being the smallest one there, I was elected to do this job and never looked forward to it. Several of the bakers would pick me up, turn me horizontal and place me in front of the oven. I would then wiggle around until I was on a rack, inside the oven. Then someone would run the rack around until I was near the bottom and could wiggle around and clean up everything. One day, the bakers yelled to me while in the oven, that they were going to lunch and closed the door. They thought that was pretty funny.

It was also my job to unload the flour truck when it came. The sacks of flour weighed as much as I did, so I learned leverage at a young age. If the driver placed the sack on my shoulders, I could stagger over to the pile and let it fall in proper order with the rest. One day, the driver decided to "fun" with me. As I approached for another sack, he threw it towards me like a bean bag. I ended up on the floor with a 100-pound sack of flour on me and covered with white flour. I think he learned new cuss words as soon as I got my breath back.

On Sundays I came in and scrubbed the restaurant that was part of the bakery. I let myself in with a key they left for me. They had a new gadget, called a television, sitting on a shelf. On Sundays, there were three channels of test patterns. I was told never to touch it. Of course, every Sunday I turned it on as I mopped the floor and cleaned the kitchen. When I was done, I returned the key to its place and locked up. I would then go around the front and look in the window to admire my work. One day, as I gazed in, I noticed the television was still on. I just locked myself out and knew I was in big trouble. As I ran home, I tried to figure out what to do now. Up the street came the owner of the bakery and my boss. I waved and tearfully told them the terrible thing I did and to my surprise they said, "Don't worry about it, we'll take care of it". I've never been so surprised or relieved in my life. I guess they liked my work. They next started driving me to another restaurant they had, and I cleaned that at night. This job definitely kept me busy. I still didn't have time to get in trouble.

At 15, I was an experienced driver and decided to use some of my savings to buy a car. I found a 1938 Plymouth coupe with a 1951 engine for $150. I was too young to have a license, so a kindly neighbor man drove the car home for me. We parked it in the vacant lot next door, and I proceeded to investigate what I had. I soon discovered it needed brakes. I bought my first special tool at this time. It was a wheel puller for a 1938 Plymouth. I still have it, because "you never know." At that time brake shoes had riveted linings, and you took off the old lining and riveted the new ones on. If you have ever looked at drum brakes, you know how complex they are compared to disc brakes. They have several springs and spacers that have to be installed perfectly to work. I changed everything one wheel at a time so I could run around the car and look at the other side to see where everything went together.

By the time I turned 16, got a license, and was finally legal, the car was ready to go. The first thing I did was take it to

"Four Wheel Brakes" to get the brakes adjusted as I wasn't confident of my adjustment. When they inspected the car, they came out to tell me "You need a new set of brakes". My first lesson in shady mechanics. I was so surprised all I could say was "That's OK, just adjust them". I then "customized" the Plymouth. It had prime painted fender skirts and fake Cadillac hub caps, that were stolen within a month. I still had to park on a hill at night as it wouldn't start with the starter when cold. Only later did I find the battery under the seat and it was low on water. Who knew?

A year later I spotted a 1941 Ford convertible in a dealer's window on Broadway in Oakland's "auto row". For $325 I got a newly painted "Palisades Grey" convertible in excellent condition. I put skirts on it, took the chrome off and filled in the holes, called "shaving the deck". I drove this for a year and never had a bit of trouble.

Someone talked me into buying a 1946 Olds two door sedan and I learned how to fix cars on that one. I replaced the engine twice. The brakes, transmission, and tires once. What a lemon. My next car was a 1939 Ford Coupe that I kept for a year.

My favorite class in High School was Physics, taught by Mr. Bartholomew. We would do experiments with beakers over flame and mix different chemicals together with some strange results. I loved it. As I was enrolled in a work-program, they called 4-4. You were supposed to go to school for four hours and then work four hours. It didn't leave much time for homework. The job I had required preparing 16mm film to be mailed to different groups where it would be run on a projector and shown on a screen, just like the movies. I would prepare the returned films by running it through my fingers as it was rewound onto another reel. I would repair broken sprockets, and sometimes broken film. That was always interesting. The film would be running through my fingers, if there was a break in the film it would go all over the room before I could stop it by pinching down on the spinning reel. Sometimes, the customer would reattach it with a straight pin. That would end up in a finger. Surprise! I would then splice it back together and continue. The reels were about 18 inches in diameter and viewing time was about half an hour. When the film was ready it would go in a shipping container, and I would place stamps and an address on it. When I was finally done, I would deliver them to the main Post Office in Berkeley and go home. Sometimes, I didn't finish until late at night.

As a result of this I found time to do my homework between classes, which irritated Mr. Bartholomew to the point he gave me a "D" grade for the term. I protested my grade, pointing out I never got lower than a "C" in tests and got mostly "B"s. He informed me I got a "D" because I did my homework between classes. I knew this was unfair, but I couldn't explain to him I was working 8 hours a day and didn't have the time. They would have kicked me out of 4-4. I could add that my classes were all "College Prep" except for A-period gym, which was mandatory. Nothing like swimming in an outdoor pool in the middle of winter at 7am.

On a rainy day in December, we were all gathered for lunch in the basement of Tech High in Oakland. There were benches around the room. My friend Joe and I lucked out and found a place to sit. The room was full of students, all races and colors, there to get out of the rain. Suddenly a couple of rough looking black guys approached and said to Joe, "Gimmee a cookie". This was not a request; it was a demand. Joe replied, "No way," and they grabbed a cookie out of his shirt pocket along with the pocket. I stood up, all 110 pounds of me, and shouted "Leave him alone." Suddenly the room was full of just black guys. This is a school where the vice principal lost his front teeth to a black group, he encountered in the basement. I knew I was dead. No doubt about it. Tom Smart, a football star on the school football team, appeared behind the instigators. Tom stood next to me in A-period gym class, and we were friends. Tom proceeded to grab the two and slammed their heads together with a sound like two coconuts being cracked. I'll never forget that sound. In a commanding voice, he said "What's the problem here fellows?" Rubbing their heads, they replied "No problem, Tom." It was Tom's best performance ever.

One class was taught in a room with rows of seats going up like a theatre. One day, we had a young substitute teacher who wasn't much older than we were. She was writing something on the blackboard, which was slate, and you wrote on it with chalk. I just couldn't resist; I made a paper airplane and threw it at the blackboard. It landed about a foot from her, and she broke the chalk. Suddenly, everybody turned to look at me. Surprised, I turned and looked at the boy behind me. He was surprised too and voiced his innocence. Luckily, no one got in trouble. I had never done anything like this before and never did it again. I felt sorry for the young teacher and wondered what made me do that. It probably bothered me more than it did her.

The paint on the Hudson was worse for wear, especially after Mom waxed it with Johnsons Floor Wax out in the sun. It looked kind of blotchy. I decided to paint the car for her. I had been hanging out at the Flying A Gas Station at 41st and Broadway and the owner allowed me to paint the car in his grease rack. I carefully sanded it down and painted it Oldsmobile green. After letting it cure for a good hour, I drove it home and let her discover it the next day. Of course, she was very surprised and happy to see it and never noticed my mishaps with the paint job. It was about this time I suspected I might be color blind as I had trouble telling new paint from the old. I finally figured out new paint went on shiny and was able to cover the whole car neatly.

My mom and I used to argue about the color of grass. I insisted it was red and she equally insisted it was green. As a child, I colored all the grass red in my coloring books. After the car paint job, I began to see she might be right. Later in life I drove 18 wheelers and needed a commercial license. At the Department of Motors Vehicles, they took your picture, and they would instruct you to stand on the red or green line for the picture. If you were going for a commercial license you stood on a different line. I would stand nearby to see which line the different people stood on to figure out where I should stand, because I couldn't tell the difference between them. As far as traffic lights, I would look for the position of the light that was on, as all lights had the red light on the top. Except in Winslow, Arizona, in the fifties. They just had two lights, with the green light on top. In the middle of the night, I stopped for the green light and when it turned red, I drove through it. The only reason I know this, is I had a buddy with me, who took notice. In 48 years of driving trucks, I never had a problem, except I had a few "streetlights" turn red on me. I was aware of my color blindness and very careful around any kind of lights.

Part 4: 1953, After High School

I graduated from Technical High School, at 43rd and Broadway, in Oakland, CA. in January, 1953, just three months after turning 17. I got a job delivering groceries at Piedmont Grocery in Oakland. Piedmont Grocery had a bakery upstairs called "Winston's Bakery". They had a "dumb waiter" elevator to deliver everything downstairs to the store. They had a newfangled gadget called a bread slicer. Now, you could buy your bread sliced.

What a great idea.

At Christmas time people would order bakery goods way ahead of time. The orders would be made up and placed on rolling racks for storage until the customer showed up. I'll never forget the good aromas at Christmas time. The floors were dark wood, which was cleaned every night with sawdust and oil. All the cans on the shelves had to be marked with the price. This was done with a rubber marker that you pressed into an ink pad and then pressed against the can's top. One press on the ink pad, one press on a can. After a while you could get a rhythm going and do it pretty fast. When you were done shopping, the cashier would look at the price on the can and enter it on the keys of the cash register. No laser to find the code in those days. Everything paid for in cash or check. No credit cards around then.

I was delivering groceries, mostly into affluent Piedmont. The store decided to find out how many customers had freezers. We were told to ask each customer, while delivering the groceries, if they had a freezer, and how large it was. After doing this a while, I happened upon a lady that misunderstood me. She thought I was trying to sell her a freezer, and what size did she want. She appeared to be ready to buy and asked me the price. I might have missed my calling.

The owner of Piedmont Grocery bought into a place in Lake County called "Bartlett Springs". They had a natural spring of mineral water that they bottled at a plant next to the springs. The grocery store owner, Mr. Skaggs, paid me extra to drive the six-wheel produce truck up to retrieve bottled water on a weekend. I drove my VW bug up there first to check it out. It was the rainy season and my friend Wayne and I came upon a muddy section on the dirt road. A tow truck had just towed a car out of the mud and offered a price to pull us through. He offered a higher price if we got stuck. I knew the VW had a flat under carriage and decided to try it. We backed up a ways and made it through with a little momentum. When we came to the stream it was flooded. I had Wayne get in the back seat for more weight over the drive wheels. We proceeded to ford the stream and water was up to the chrome strip on the side of the car. The engine had to be under water, but it didn't skip a beat. It leaked one drop of water through a hole in the "firewall" where a lever came through from the gas tank which you would flip when you ran out of gas. It held a gallon in reserve because there was no gas gauge. The VW had weather stripping so good you had to roll the window down a little to close the door. No wonder it didn't leak. I reported back to the boss we should wait for spring before attempting a trip to get bottled water.

I would start out by picking up a load of glass bottles at a plant in Antioch and then drive up to Bartlett Springs and unload. Then, the operator would drive his car up to the side of the bottling plant and run jumper cables through a hole in the wall and connect them to a Model A engine and transmission. There was no electricity up there. He would start the engine and put it in gear attached to a huge one-cylinder diesel engine. This turned the diesel engine over enough to eventually start it. It required holding a blow torch on a warm-up plug in the diesel's head. The diesel had two six foot in diameter flywheels. As soon as it warmed up, he would connect it to a generator that was about four feet high. This would produce electricity, so he could start the bottling plant. He would fill the bottles I brought and I would reload the truck and deliver them back to the store the next morning. It was quite an operation. The last 16 miles into the plant was a dirt road that forded a stream twice and went over a summit to get there. One trip it snowed, and I'd never driven in snow. I was scared but very carefully made it out. A fan belt broke, so I tied a rope in its place which worked long enough to find another belt. When I had a flat tire, no one would touch the truck's wheel. It had split rims you had to separate with a crowbar, repair the inner tube and put back together with a sledgehammer. This was tricky as the rim was hard to get back in the slot and could explode off the wheel with enough force to hurt something or somebody. I was able to do it safely but was scared the whole time. Back then they had no "tubeless" tires. Car tires were difficult enough to fix but didn't have the split rims that trucks did.

On one trip, I was stopped by a cop just after exiting the Carquinez Bridge near Vallejo. I was too young, by one year, to have a commercial license to drive a truck of that size and weight. He asked what I was hauling. I told him about the benefits of Bartlett Water and that it would make hair grow on your chest 10 feet long, among other things. This got him laughing, as a result he ended up giving me only a warning and told me to get the proper license, which I did, a year later.

About this time, I was also working nights in the Flying A Gas Station on Broadway and 41st Street. This was after working my day job at Piedmont Grocery. I would get a percentage of the gas sales; the amount of sales went up as I really tried hard to please customers in this full-service gas station. Forget self-service. Forget credit cards. Everything was handled in cold cash, even at 25 cents a gallon.

In those days, we cleaned your windshield, checked the oil, and offered green stamps, to be redeemed on stuff like pots and pans. Sometimes, we even gave away pots and pans for a certain amount of gas sales. One customer always came to our station as we would clean the driver's door for him. He chewed tobacco and made a mess spitting out the window. We also changed oil and actually lubricated the grease fittings on your car. Those days are long gone.

The station had a type of gas pump I wish they had today. You could dial in the octane you wanted, and the price would automatically change to suit the octane. It worked well for the old hot rodder trick of advancing the timing and using the octane you needed to prevent "pinging" as well as pick up a little more horsepower. Pinging is also known as detonation and cars made today have a "knock sensor" to prevent that. Back then if you ignored the "pinging" you could blow a hole in a piston.

This gas station was of a type common in those days, in having glass walls all around the room where you displayed oil and batteries, etc. One Thanksgiving night, a friendly lady who lived on the second floor of an apartment house next door, looked down with pity at me in this glass room and decided to bring me a full Thanksgiving dinner on a tray. What a treat for a teenage kid with his first apartment.

I lived one block away from the station. One night someone broke the door of the station and entered looking for the cash drawer. We "cleverly" hid it at closing time behind a case of oil. The police arrived at my place in the middle of the night after calling the gas station owner, who lived out of town. I dressed and followed them down to the station and showed them where the thief had missed finding the money. Pretty exciting for a teenager.

One night I was running the station. A guy came in driving a big black Cadillac, with two gorgeous women in the back seat dressed in furs. He started calling my friend and I "Champ". "I'm looking for Phil, Champ." I explained that Phil, the owner of the station, went home, and left me in charge. "Well, fill it up, Champ, with premium." He got out a roll of money about three inches in diameter and gave me a tip, for doing a good job cleaning the windows. That almost never happened. "Thanks, Champ. Tell Phil, Max stopped by." And away he went. I asked my friend "Who the heck was that?" He replied, "That was Max Baer, heavy weight champion." I didn't have a clue who he was. Later, I learned, he and Phil grew up together, in West Oakland.

One day a tenant in a nearby apartment house came into the station and asked the owner, Phil, if he knew a good driver who could drive his new Mercury and him, up to his property in Lake County. Phil suggested me, we agreed on a price, and away we went. Once there, I discovered it was an old farmhouse with a barn. He wanted to exercise some of the machinery and showed me how to start a small bulldozer and several other machines. I really enjoyed learning how to operate them. Little did I know that 35 years later I would have a job that included operating the same machines, only bigger.

Back at the gas station a customer, named Sam, asked if I was interested in driving cars for him. He was an "Insurance Adjuster". His specialty was repossessing cars. He needed someone to ride along with him to drive the cars he repossessed. I loved driving, so I agreed. We were basically stealing cars. I learned how to break into a car without actually breaking things and to "hotwire" the ignition. Most cars were just given up by the owner, but quite a few we actually stole, usually in the middle of the night. When we were done, the adjuster would notify the police.

One repossession that comes to mind is a car we tied a rope to and Sam towed it out of a garage, up the driveway and around the corner, while I steered the car, going backwards past an open bedroom window, in the middle of the night. We were in West Oakland, a tough place to be in those days.

Another time, the car we picked up had bullet holes in the back. The owner had just robbed a bank and was at large.

The worst one was in a remote area outside Moraga where there were no streetlights and it was very dark. We attempted to steal a car that turned out to be owned by a deputy sheriff. As I held a flashlight for Sam, while he attempted to break in, another pair of shoes appeared in the light. I raised the light up past his gun to a badge and knew we were in trouble. Luckily, Sam was able to talk us out of our predicament. All this ended when Sam got a girlfriend.

A couple doors up Broadway, from the gas station, there was a repair shop. They had a beat up '36 Ford coupe, that they raced at the Pacheco dirt track. They called it "Hard Top" racing. They would tow it up through the Caldecot Tunnel, into Contra Costa County and on to Pacheco. I used to ride along in my "free time", of which I didn't have much. On this night, the pickup hauling the hardtop couldn't quite make the grade. While we were still moving, slowly, up the Caldecot grade, the person who was going to race the coupe got out on the running board, climbed over the truck bed, and into the race car. He then put the race car in gear, started it, and proceeded to push the pickup through the tunnel. When we got there, we had to qualify the car for the race. There were always more cars available than could race at one time, so you "qualified" by being in the top ten cars. This night I begged to qualify the car for them. I never drove on a dirt track before, but I observed how drivers did it. They finally relented and to everybody's surprise, I beat out several other cars and qualified the car. At this point I wanted to race it, and they were agreeable as I did a good job qualifying. At this point a race official took a good look at me and asked my age. In those days, you had to be a minimum of 18 years of age to race. I was so disappointed that they wouldn't let me race. Now they have guys younger than that driving Formula One race cars. Maybe people figured something out over the years.

I had my own apartment by now and actually had three cars for a short time. One was a '39 Ford Coupe which I bought already customized with tuck and roll Naugahyde upholstery and a molded-in body, painted metallic blue. It was gorgeous, but I wanted more. I removed the engine, transmission and rear end and changed everything. I sold the '41 Mercury engine, for $25, and I found a '49 Olds V-8 from a wreck and managed to shoehorn it into the coupe. This necessitated moving the battery to the trunk

Lost Child Found

for lack of space under the hood. Higher speed Lincoln Zephyr gears went into the transmission and higher speed gears went into the rear end. Reversed Buick rims went on the back with big Buick tires. This gave the coupe a "rake", the rear was higher than the front. Perfect. A great German mechanic on 40th Street, Clarence Bebidorf, let me have space in his shop to build the car. In return, I bought parts from him, and he did welding when needed. I occasionally would work on a customer's car for him. I found a great radio out of a Pierce Arrow. It came in three sections, and I mounted a 15" speaker behind the seat on a shelf under the rear window. It had great sound for a radio built before "HiFi" FM or stereo.

When I sold the '39 coupe to my best friend, Bob Higgins, he hopped up the engine more, and it turned into a real fast car. He was followed one night, in the Mojave Desert, by a California Highway Patrol. He was doing 90 mph, and the cop put on his red light. Bob knew the road because his father lived nearby. He figured the cop was too far away to read his license, and he could lose him. He proceeded to do just that. At that time, The CHP was using Dodge D500 cars that would do 133 mph. So, the coupe ran away from a very fast car.

'39 Ford Coupe – Sperry Family Collection

Lost Child Found

While I was building the '39 Ford, I drove a completely worn out '38 Ford roadster with a "rumble seat", now a very rare car. For those not born in the nineteenth century, a rumble seat was another seat, completely removed from the front seat. Instead of a trunk lid, there was another lid that opened so that it formed the back of the rumble seat. There were steps in the body to enable a person to climb into the seat. Once in, you were facing the front with the windshield a long way away. If the top was up, you were looking at the rear window. It worked great for two couples at a drive-in movie. That's another lost function that was always fun. You could drive to the movies, park your car, facing the huge screen, and never get out of your car.

Back then it was a $35 junker. It had power. But when I street raced anyone there would be water, steam, and oil creeping up the windshield. It smoked out the back through dual "smitty" straight pipes so much that when it stopped smoking, I knew it was out of oil. One night I pulled into a gas station and said, "Give me 5 quarts of oil and check the gas."

When I got the '38, the mechanical brakes were completely out of adjustment. I found out, one night, as I was coming down a hill in the rain. I put on the brakes and suddenly spun completely around facing the other way. I actually paid money to have them adjusted. One of the few expenses for this car for a whole year.

This car had a gasoline fired heater that was called "Tropic Air", or something like that. It was great. On the coldest morning you would have instant heat. The radio was also very good. Although you better have the engine running if you listened to it for more than ten minutes or else the car battery would go dead.

I painted the car with black primer paint: a common thing done to a "rod". The rag top was really a rag, but I managed to find something to spray on it, in hopes of improving the looks.

The clutch started to slip so I loosened the floorboards, which were real wood, to let the clutch pedal come up a little more. It worked. (Henry Ford specified the dimensions of the boards used to make crates to contain parts being sold to Ford. He would use them for floorboards.)

I was active with a great group of kids, from different parts of town. We would meet on a Wednesday night for "Prayer Meeting", at a Methodist Church on Telegraph, near MacArthur. Not much "Prayer Meeting" was done but we had a great time. One night we were all going out to eat, and one of the kids had his dad's new car. He was afraid he would leave me behind, in my worn out '38 Ford. A girl assured him, saying "You won't get away from Paul." My reputation was growing.

I got a ticket for loud exhaust and temporarily "fixed" it by shoving steel wool up the exhaust pipes. I then drove into the police garage and revved up the engine. The police inspector took one look and asked if I shoved steel wool up the tail pipes. I replied, "They're quiet now." He let me off, but he knew what I had done. It didn't hardly run that way. I used a coat hanger to pull the steel wool out as soon as I could.

The body was so worn, there were cracks coming from the bottom corners of the rumble seat, but everything still worked.

One morning I gave a hitchhiker a ride. As we came to a corner, I didn't shift down to second, but lugged the engine a little as I went around the corner. The engine didn't like that and suddenly the transmission shifted into second gear, all by itself. I was as surprised as the hitchhiker. "What was that?" he asked. I replied, "Automatic transmission," and we both laughed.

I finally blew a head gasket on the '38. I removed the heads and ground them down to level again, using a big piece of glass and valve grinding paste. It took a while, but it worked. The engine came out with higher compression and went even faster.

I had a girlfriend in Piedmont, and I visited her one night. On the way down the hill, the exhaust was doing its usual backfiring, crackle and pop. A Piedmont cop pulled me over. I was sure it was about the straight pipes. He surprised me by pointing out that the tail-lights weren't working. I kicked the rear fender, and they came back on. He looked surprised. I said, "Anything else?" He looked confused and told me: "Get out of Piedmont and don't come back." That's the kind of car it was.

On the fourth of July, I traveled to another town to watch the fireworks. On the way back, I was going the speed limit at the head of a long string of traffic. I was very aware of Police presence in the area and was going slow so I wouldn't get pulled over. Alas, the lights weren't that bright at low speed. I got pulled over and ticketed for the lights. They told me not to drive the car until daylight. I guess they thought I would just walk home. I decided to stay in the car, as I couldn't lock it and I had all my tools and a paint sprayer in the car. As they patrolled back my way, they spotted me in the car and stopped and asked what I was doing. I explained I didn't want to leave my stuff in the car. They then asked if I knew the way home on back streets. I proceeded to tell them what route I would take, and they told me to go home. Soon after, I sold the car, mostly because there was no way I could make the lights any brighter. When the '39 Coupe was finished, I sold the '38 convertible for $35 and came out even.

The '39 Ford coupe had twin "baby" spotlights, that came in handy one night, when the headlights quit working.

I had a trailer hitch connected to the rear bumper and reinforced directly to the frame. This made for a very strong bumper. One night while waiting at a red light, I was rear ended by a man in a Plymouth. The whole front of his car was pushed in, with not a scratch on the coupe. With the "rake", on the coupe, the bumper was even with his grill and front fenders. When the police came, the other driver claimed my brake lights didn't work. I replied, "They did, before you hit me." I got in the coupe and put on the brakes. Luckily, they worked. That killed his story.

Another night, after making a "burger run", to the fast-food joint on 22nd in Oakland, I was on my way back to the gas station on Broadway when all of a sudden the Ford quit running. There was a cop behind me, so I got out and approached him for help. He wasn't interested and drove off. That's when I noticed smoke coming from under the car. Luckily, I had a flashlight and crawled under the car to check it out. The battery in the trunk had a long cable going to the starter which shorted out on the frame and ignited some grease. I was able to disconnect the cable and put the fire out; traffic continued to pass me by with no offer of help. When I finished and got the car started again, I noticed a bad burn on the back of my hand. I drove myself to Kaiser Hospital Emergency and they cleaned it up and bandaged it for me. I still have a scar there. Now it looks like an "aging" spot.

When I finished the '39 coupe it would do 60 mph in first gear and 90 mph in second. I never wound it out in third. When I raced, I would have to hold it in second or it would pop out of gear, a common Ford "trait," and when I reached 90, it would get hot, and lock up and I had to hold the clutch in until it cooled down. If I couldn't beat someone in second, it was all over anyway.

I kept the coupe about a year and never got a ticket. By this time, I was out of high school and working. I sold the coupe to my friend, Bob Higgins, and went looking for a brand-new car.

First, I tried a Willys. It was a small car and I liked the size. I sat in it and started to adjust the rear-view mirror and it came off in my hand. When I tried to open the door, the handle came off. I decided against that car.

I also considered at a weird looking import which was just being imported into the country from Germany. After taking in the weird shape, I noticed how well it was put together. Everything fit properly, had a nice finish to it, and operated as it should. It only had 36 horsepower, so I wondered how it would drive. A salesman was happy to demonstrate that. He drove up on sidewalks and off again to demonstrate the "torsion bar suspension" and the 4-wheel independent suspension. It had a four-speed transmission on the floor and steered very easily and was sporty to drive. I ended up buying my first Volkswagen, one of many more to follow.

Then I started getting tickets. If you went around a corner fast the rear end would slide out and you would correct and get around the corner faster. The police did not appreciate or understand the fun this was. This started a love affair with "V" cars for many years to come.

The next year, I switched to a Volvo 444 that looked like a small version of a '40 Ford 2-door sedan. It had twice the power of the VW and a "bullet proof" engine. I ended up having "V" cars for many years. I began racing the Volvo in Autocross where you race against the clock on a closed course. These courses were usually at a parking lot or an old airport. I pulled the engine and made my own head gasket out of .010 dead soft copper to raise the compression. I tried to get a speed cam from Ed Iskenderian in L.A.; he told me he could make it idle lumpy, but not go any faster. Again, Volvo got there first. I also had it balanced. The only thing not balanced was a washer, on the front of the crankshaft. I don't think all this work made the car go any faster. Volvo had already made it pretty fast and "bullet proof". I won six races in sedan class that year and got the season's trophy from the Northern California Corvette Club, who sponsored the races. 61 years later, I discovered an article in the Oakland Tribune, that covered this event, with my name as the winner in "Sedan class".

Around 1957, Chevy Corvette came out with fuel injection. This improved the performance of the engine dramatically. The only other American cars, with fuel injection, were race cars and dragsters, at great expense. To modify an engine required changing to new heads and intake manifold. Very expensive. I came up with an idea for modifying the engine without changing heads or manifold. I called it a "fuel injected spark plug". The idea was to introduce the fuel and ignition through the existing spark plug hole in the head. My uncle Charles had a small machine shop in Oakland, where he made "piston expanders" during the war. This was a springlike device that would expand the piston enough to further the life of your engine for a while. During the war you couldn't get your engine rebuilt for lack of material and mechanics. Everything was used for the war effort.

I approached him (in 1957) for advice; he agreed to go in with me and share everything 50-50. He proposed a patent search first, to make sure we wouldn't infringe on someone else's patent and invite a lawsuit. We paid 50-50 for the patent search and discovered 23 patents we might infringe on. The latest was a vice president of General Motors. So, my idea wasn't as "far out" as I thought it might be. We dropped the idea. I discovered twenty years later that Opel of Germany (owned by GM) had actually built an engine with that feature, and it worked. By that time, fuel injection was common in engines, and the idea was apparently dropped again.

About this time, I switched jobs, going from the grocery store to a new dairy just starting. It was partly owned by the Piedmont Grocery, so I had a "heads up" about it before hand. They were going to call it Gold'n Rich milk, but settled for Valley Gold milk, produced by Gold'n Rich Corporation. They copied the name of a dairy in Albuquerque, NM. Among other owners there was a co-op chain of grocers that were all over the Bay Area. I drove truck #2, a ten-wheel, three-axle Chevy van with an insulated body, with a four-speed transmission and a two-speed rear end. It was the biggest truck I had ever driven. We got the milk off the truck with a hook, one stack at a time, using a power lift gate. I learned much later that other employees were betting I wouldn't last on the job, because I was kind of small for the job. I went from weighing 130 pounds to my lifelong working weight of 165 pounds very quickly. I ended up being there 24 years, except for four years in the military.

Part 5: 1958, Beating the Draft

The draft was still on so I decided I better do something about it. I had to sell the Volvo and then joined the Air Force. I got there just in time, as my draft notice came while I was in basic training. I told the sergeant I had to leave, and he assured me he would take care of it.

After scoring 95% on Mechanical and 95% in Electronics, I purposely failed Administrative. I was given a book full of colored dots. I aced it, getting most of the numbers correct. That's when they told me the only people who could read that book were color blind. So much for Electronics.

The next test was for ability to learn a foreign language. I passed and was to be sent to Yale, Harvard, or Monterey Russian Language School. The Air Force would not say what the job would be, but it required a very high security clearance and was in "intelligence". This position was rated pretty high. I was sent to the dentist, while in Basic Training. The only other people going to the dentist were officers who were going to be trained as pilots.

While I waited, they sent out a notice to see if our parents were from certain countries behind the iron curtain, the iron curtain being countries under the control of Russia. Of course, I announced I was half Czech. That's what it says on my adoption papers. At that point they kicked me out of that job, despite my complaints. They then decided to place me in Jet Engine School. The Air Force was switching to jet bombers in 1958 and they needed a new generation of mechanics to work on them.

I ended up in Basic for 16 weeks. I was assigned to a fearsome training instructor, whose nick name was El Toro. He was Mexican and fierce in appearance. He had a reputation. After being with him for a few weeks, we thought he was a pussy cat. One example happened on a rare August rainy day in Texas. He told us the roller-skating rink was owned by the Base Commander. He was instructed to have us all go roller skating, or we could stay in the barracks and smoke. Guess which one we chose?

There was a tradition that each bay would have an arm-wrestling champion who would compete with the upper bay, with the winner becoming the champion of the 140-man barracks. After winning the bottom bay, I had to go up against a very large black kid from Harrisburg, PA. He outweighed me by 40 pounds and was built like a boxer. We rolled around on the floor for a while, neither of us able to put down the other. Suddenly, my foot contacted the wall and somehow, I had just enough leverage to put him down. This was all done in a friendly manner and there were no hard feelings, and we became good friends while we were there.

I was the oldest recruit, being 23, while most were 17 or 18. When they inspected us every morning, I had more of a beard than most. Some weren't even shaving yet. I would shave as close as I could each morning and if they asked, "When did you shave", I would say, "Last night, Sir." They would then tell me to shave in the morning. It was a little game we played.

I knew I chose the right service when one day we were out camping in what they called "Survivor Training". It was a hot August day in Texas when a sudden unexpected rainstorm came by. We were enjoying it inside our tents when they decided to cancel "Survivor Training" because of the rain. A whole bunch of "Pith" helmets got mashed up as we threw everything on a flatbed truck. This was watched over by an officer with a service issued umbrella.

Those of us waiting for a school to open became better and better at marching, since that's all we did. Everywhere we went, we marched as a group. Usually, the T.I. would call out commands to keep everybody together. We dug in our heels so much, people would come out to see what the noise was. The T.I. never had to say a word. I ended up being in Basic so long that when I left for trade school, they awarded me my first stripe. This turned out to be a huge advantage.

While waiting for my turn at Jet school I was made a "Night CQ Runner". This involved sitting in a chair in the office all night in case someone had to be summoned. One night I read in the paper that there was a fire at an Air Force Russian Language School dormitory that killed everybody in it. It could have been me, except for my announcing my Czech ancestry.

I learned if you scored 95% on your final test, they would give you a ride in a jet fighter. Sounded good to me. Alas, I only scored 94.5%. I failed the torque wrench test; they used a pound-inch wrench that I had never heard of. It must be used making watches or something. I was supposed to tighten a bolt to 15-**pound-inches**. I was thinking 15-**pound-feet** which isn't very much either. I blew right by 15-pound-inches and lost my plane ride.

When I graduated, I ended up in SAC (Strategic Air Command) under General Curtis LeMay, working on B-52s and KC135 tankers, a military version of the Boeing 707 airliner. They were brand new, taking the place of prop driven B-36s and their KC-97 tankers. I was assigned to Travis Air Base in California. My roommate was Robby Robbins from Tennessee; we became good friends.

B-52 Stratofortress – Courtesy of DefenseMediaNetwork.com

I couldn't afford the auto insurance they required to park on the base, so I sold my trusty '52 Chevy, and bought a used BSA twin cylinder motorcycle. It was a great bike and I put 7000 miles on it one summer. I had a girlfriend at Lake Tahoe, and I could put 1000 miles a week on it without trying.

A buddy from the base and I took off one morning for a trip to some curvy roads I knew about above Oakland. As we came down Old Tunnel Road back into town, we started into a curve side-by-side, when suddenly we were right in the middle of an oil spill. Ed's bike went down, and he ended up sliding along on the pavement. I was right beside him, trying not to run over him, and instinctively put my right foot down on the pavement, and managed to recover. My boot landed in oil, which was probably lucky, as it didn't stick to the pavement. It was a glorious dirt track maneuver made on oily pavement, and it worked. Ed's bike had a ground-down place on one handlebar but was otherwise OK. His leather jacket was oily, but everything else was OK. We continued on our way, and kept an eye on the road, more than before.

One night, as I was approaching the toll booth at the Carquinez Bridge, the throttle cable broke. The throttle was at highway speed, and I couldn't slow down enough, even using the brakes. Luckily there was a kill button front and center, and I used that, off and on, as I came up to the toll booth. The toll taker could see what was happening and crouched down in case I ran into the booth. I managed to get it stopped, right next to the booth, and paid my toll. He then stopped all traffic while I wheeled the now-disabled bike to the side of the road. I discovered the front brake cable was identical to the throttle cable so I used it for the throttle until I was able to get another cable. I always carried a couple tools, which came in handy this trip.

I sold the bike, when I found a cheaper way to get insurance, and bought a much-used VW bug. It had been used by a newspaper carrier and had a couple mashed up fenders, but it ran OK. I installed new fenders and had an aircraft painter put a beautiful metallic blue paint job on it.

I found a fellow in Oakland, that agreed to insure me for a cheaper price, because I was in the military. I ended up using him to insure future cars and several houses, right up to the time he died, twenty years later.

When I got an extra part-time job, working grave shift at a produce warehouse in Berkeley, I bought a '54 Ford pickup because I discovered I could take marginal produce from the warehouse on a Friday that they would dump on Monday. They were glad to see me take it. I would then sell it up at the base for a reasonable price and for a while I had quite a business going.

They assigned me to Jet Engine Test Cell, where we tested engines from our build-up shop. There are several different configurations of engines on a B-52, one has a hydraulic pump, another a constant speed drive running an alternator. If an engine quit on an aircraft, we could replace it with one from our shop. So, we always had spare engines ready to hang on aircraft. That's exactly how the engines are attached to the aircraft. There is one main bolt, hanging under the wing, where you attach the engine. There are also two pins on each end, to further attach the engine, but all of the weight is on that one bolt. It is a very special bolt, made of some serious metal. The nut is torqued on with a six-foot long torque wrench, to a very high figure.

One day they planned an "en masse" takeoff of all the B-52s on the base. I smuggled my 8mm movie camera into Test Cell in my toolbox and planned on photographing the event from our great location next to the runway. Wouldn't you know it, the wind changed direction that day, and I was stuck photographing all the smoke as they took off in the other direction.

The B-52 has "bicycle" landing gear, with outrigger wheels to stabilize it when the wings are full of fuel. The aircraft has the capability of landing slightly turned into the wind. It's really something to see. They look like they will crash, as they are landing, while turned slightly either way. It's a great way to deal with side winds and seems to work. After they touch down, the body straightens out and it looks like a normal aircraft.

The only other aircraft I know of with "bicycle" gear is the U-2 spy plane. Its outrigger wheels fall off as they take off. When they land, it is at such a low speed, the wing tips don't touch the ground enough to damage them. It has so much lift that sometimes they have to kill the engine to get the plane to touch down.

After working at Jet Engine Test Cell, I switched to working on the line. I was on swing shift and loved it. We would be called to start engines for other shops, but mostly did engine trims, like a carburetor adjustment on a car. After work, I would drive to the produce warehouse in Berkeley, starting at 1:00am. I usually worked until seven. I also was running cars to and from the Port of Oakland. There was a place, off base, that would ship a G.I.'s car overseas and back again. By Friday people would ask me "What are you doing for eyes?" I guess by then they got kind of red.

I had a "hardship" payment coming out of my check and it didn't leave me much to live on, so I worked more. My hardship payment went to my mom, so she could afford a payment on an old house she bought in East Oakland. I wasn't alone. Especially if a G.I. was married, he had another job. At the produce warehouse, I loaded our trucks for delivery to grocery stores the next day, and also received and unloaded produce trucks making deliveries to the warehouse. I did such a good job, the company laid off a couple of full-time workers. Finally, the union advised the company to lay off the part-time guy next. So, I worked myself out of a job. It was the only time I was ever fired from a job.

I grabbed a little sleep, whenever and wherever I could and was still able to perform my various jobs to everybody's satisfaction.

This was during the "Cold War". People didn't realize it but we had B-52s flying 24/7, with nuclear weapons, down the coast of Russia, in case they tried something. Our base had their quota of bombers to keep flying. We also had KC-135 tankers that supported the bombers. All this required a tremendous amount of maintenance. The J-57 engine was also used by the F-102 Interceptors that were at Travis. We maintained them at Test Cell, testing the operation and afterburner after they came out of their shop. The Jet Engine Test Cell was located by the runway in case an engine had a problem. We had a couple start shaking and blow the back of the engine off. We saw fire trucks a number of times. They taught me how to run up the engines for testing. Soon after I learned that skill, we had an engine start vibrating. Everybody watched the instruments climbing and suddenly it exploded. Everyone ran outside our reinforced control room to see the action, except for me. I was still at the controls of a now ruined engine. My training kicked in and I shut off the engine and operated the air starter. This "blew" the fire out. Finally, I was able to go outside, to find many fire trucks around and a Major looking in the tailpipe. I ran over and pushed him away. I then explained to him the fire could easily reignite and a fire ball would come out the tailpipe. He looked kind of ashen and thanked me.

In their wisdom the motor pool offered a 50-passenger bus for the six of us to drive out to Test Cell. I think they figured no one would know how to drive the thing except for me, and they were right. I drove trucks before I enlisted and the bus was no problem. It was either that or an open "tug" pulling an open passenger trailer, not fun in the rain.

The Warrant Officer in charge would often ask us if we were planning on reenlisting. Because of the low pay offered and uncertain job opportunities most replied no. I learned quickly if you said that, you were taken off the promotion list. I decided I would be undecided, and as a result, I finally got my third stripe.

On one occasion, we were doing an engine trim on a B-52, and I was in the cockpit, in the right seat. We went through the engine idle speed and maximum power setting, which you did according to the barometric pressure and ambient temperature. We were starting to test the water injection settings, which they only used during takeoff. As I went to turn on water injection on the right wing, the four engines on the left wing caught fire. A switch in the fuselage water tank had failed and allowed water to the engines when they weren't up to speed. I fell back on my training and immediately called "Travis Tower" on the radio. "Travis Tower, this is aircraft 123 on spot 456. We have four engines on fire on the left wing. Request fire support." I then pulled the throttles on those four engines to stop and turned on the four engine starters. This would force air through the engines and literally blow the fire out. When I finally looked out the window of the cockpit, there were 16 fire trucks and emergency equipment in front of the aircraft. I was commended for my actions and it was my training that saved the day.

On another occasion we had a starter blow up. The starters were run by air, either from another engine that was running or from the ground cart. They turned 200,000 RPM and you didn't want to stand at the side of them. One night, as we were starting engines, one of the starters blew apart and I was looking out the window of the cockpit as the impeller blew through the case and took off in a red-hot blaze across the tarmac at a very high rate of speed.

On swing shift, we were given a little slack in how we did things as there was no "Brass" around. We developed a method of trimming engines that was speedy and accurate. We would start all the engines and go to number one and say three things to the man on the ground turning the trim screws on the engines. In the cockpit you would say "Up", "Down" and "Hold". When the engine was trimmed to target, you would notify the man on the ground: "Down on one, up on two", and go to the next engine. This was twice as fast as the Day Shift did it because we bypassed hooking up the test instrument to each engine and used the EPR gauge in the cockpit instead. EPR is "Engine Pressure Ratio" and there's one for each engine in the cockpit. It basically measures the power output of each engine. We would also adjust the manual linkage used to connect the throttles in the cockpit to each engine. The result was having the pilot at altitude be able to set his throttles according to the EPR gauges and have the throttles all even across the board. Before we started this method, we tested many EPR gauges against our instrument and found they were consistently accurate. I had one crew chief complain because he noticed we weren't doing it by the book. He let me know he would turn me in if he wasn't satisfied. Instead, he started asking for my crew when he needed work on his plane. It turned out his pilots raved about the trim we had done and wanted us back when needed.

One night we were getting ready to change a C.S.D. (Constant Speed Drive) which ran an alternator. It was not a priority, and we weren't enthusiastic about doing it.

There was unusually heavy aircraft activity that night. Our sergeant came by and declared "they" wanted this plane ready to fly quickly, as we were at war. With the activity going on we believed him, and I told my crew, "Let's do it." At this point our sergeant laughed and said he was joking. I told him I didn't like him joking about something like that. I then told him my crew and I are going to take the rest of the night off, and we did. He never pulled that on us again.

We were called out to a B-52 for an engine run on a remote launching pad. When we got there, we were surprised to see a large group standing around the bomb bay looking at a strange looking bomb we never saw before. It was still on the ground and hadn't been loaded into the bomb bay. There were a lot of guards with their dogs and weapons at the ready. A lot of "Brass" was there along with some civilians, which we never saw on the line. We had to wait until they loaded the weapon and everyone cleared out and we proceeded to run engines.

Some 50 years later, after I was retired, my wife and I attended one of our "Aviation Club" meetings to hear a talk from a club member, Paul Price, whom we knew. He proceeded to tell some of his working memories from when he was a Nuclear Scientist. He was recently declassified and could finally tell his family, and anybody else, what he used to do. Part of it was building and testing nuclear weapons. He had some slides and suddenly I recognized one. It was the aircraft from that day long ago at Travis. He and his team had built this thing and they loaded it on our B-52 and later flew somewhere over the Pacific Ocean and dropped it. The test was a success and 50 years later I got to hear about it. After the meeting, I approached Paul to check out where and when this took place and sure enough it was Travis AFB in 1960, and I was standing within 25 feet from him. It was an amazing moment.

At Travis, we always had B-52s on the Alert Pad ready to go at a moment's notice. We also supported the mission of having a B-52 flying down the coast of Russia at all times. The mission was called "Operation Chrome Dome". One night, one of our support aircraft had an engine "hang" at start up. They called me out and I discovered the six-inch wide pressure relief valve on the side of the compressor was hung open. It was supposed to be closed at start up, open at idle, and closed again at speed. This one was wide open. This required an engine change and the engine sent back to overhaul. The Officer in charge told me this was a top priority aircraft and asked if I could get it going anyway. There was an emergency fix you could try which is pretty crude but might work. I told him I could try. As they turned the starter on, I crawled up in the cowling and placed my black leather cap over the relief valve opening and held it down as hard as I could. I knew eventually I would be blown out of the cowling, but the engine might start. It did start, and I was blown out of the cowling, losing my headset as I fell. The engine worked normally now that it was started, and the aircraft flew the mission. I guess I was praised at the time, but I couldn't hear for a week after the incident. If we had been in a "hot" war instead of the "cold" war, I probably would have gotten a medal.

When I left the Air Force, I had about three weeks leave on the books, so they ran my paperwork and told me to come back and sign out at the end of my leave. During this time the "Cuban Missile Crisis" occurred. I've talked to others that were about to be discharged at that time and every one of them was extended until the crisis was over. Luckily, they didn't touch me, apparently because the paperwork had already been done. That was good for me, as I was already back on the job I had before enlisting. I applied for a job at United Airlines and was offered work in the "Hot Section Shop". This required taking apart the combustion part of the engine which was a dirty, sooty job. Workers sometimes looked like coal miners at the end of a shift. I was spoiled from working the flight line and declined. It worked out that was a good choice, as United had a few strikes and layoffs along the way and finally declared bankruptcy and cut retiree's pensions in half before they went back to business as usual.

I went back to work at the dairy, called "Gold'n Rich", where I worked before enlisting.

Part 6: 1962, The Gold'n Rich Years

Along the way I married, and we had three daughters, Colleen, Linda, and Karen. After about 14 years I became a single parent, raising my daughters despite having a job with long and sometimes unusual hours. They probably wouldn't let me do that now. My wife had mental health problems for most of our marriage. After many years of treatment, she felt well enough to get a job, and told me, in between moving to a brand-new house, that she wanted a divorce. I didn't fight it, but suggested I have custody of the girls, and occupancy of the house, to give her a better chance of being successful.

Her mental illness showed itself in the second year of our marriage. Thereafter, for twelve years we saw many doctors in many places at great expense. We moved from Oakland to the suburbs, thinking that would help. Then, back to the city in Albany. That didn't help either. We decided to try the suburbs again and bought a new house in Martinez. Right in the middle of moving, she decided she wanted a divorce. I suggested that we complete the move and see how it goes.

After a year, she had a job, and felt good enough about herself, that she wanted a divorce again. We talked with an attorney; it was decided she would get most of the furniture and I would pay her money for several years and I would keep the house and three kids with the understanding she would get half the value of the house when our youngest turned eighteen.

I had resisted divorce, because of how I felt when my adopted parents got divorced. At the time, I was convinced it was my fault, and my mother and I ended up living in another town, in the basement of a church. It happened suddenly. One day my dad was there. The next day he was gone, and I was told to choose the toys I wanted to keep that would fit in a medium-size box. The rest was buried in the backyard. Away went my electric Greyhound bus and the semi-truck and trailer that my dad had made for me out of wood, and many other treasures. I kept my Lionel train though. I still have it. I never saw my friends in the neighborhood again.

When divorce happened to me, I fought to keep my daughters and all their stuff in their own house, in their own room, and still be with their same friends in the same school. I think it helped them.

Then started the hardest thing I have ever done. I became a single parent and had to figure out how to raise three girls, feed them, clothe them, keep them active in school activities, all while working as a truck driver, sometimes late at night. One of my girls got a ride to a function at school, in a semi. Right away, I assured them they were not at fault and answered all their questions.

I learned how to cook three main dishes which would last a couple of days. I even made biscuits on Sunday morning. I cooked a turkey at Thanksgiving and had people over for dinner. We all shopped together for food and clothes, and everybody was happy about it. I made up a list of chores they could do for pay, just like I did (with no pay). Forget allowances. I helped them get jobs and taught them how to save money and buy their own ten-speed bikes. They also bought their own cars. I knew they would be proud of their things and would take better care of them and be more responsible. I also taught them that when they worked, to do the best they could. That way no one could complain about their work. If they did, that was their problem. To this day, they thank me for teaching them how to work.

Soon, Gold'n Rich decided to go with diesel trucks instead of the old gas rigs we were driving. I was given the first diesel tractor, which was much used, but was a huge improvement over the old gas engine trucks. My truck was an experimental White Truck owned by P.I.E. (Pacific Intermountain Express). It was one of the first fiberglass bodied cabs with most controls operated by air. It was a two-axle cab with another axle we added for weight capacity. The clutch, the windshield wipers, the gear shift, and of course the brakes were air operated. The gear shift was about 6-inches tall and gated, like a Ferrari. Curiously, the steering was not power anything. Everything worked as designed but the truck literally had a million miles on it. The seat was just a cushion sitting basically on the frame, but the suspension was perfect, and it had a nice ride. Later trucks always had an air-operated seat that would go up and down and even back and forth on a slider, trying to make the ride easier on the driver. My first diesel truck was a White. Next was an International and finally a White-Freightliner. In later jobs I usually drove a Freightliner. They were finally owned by Mercedes, after at least three name changes.

The milk was loaded onto the trucks on pallets that held 36 cases of 12 half gallons each. The whole thing weighed about a ton. They bought a new larger ramp to go between the truck and the dock. The old one had a lip that rested on the dock with the top of the ramp filed down. This caused the transport wheels to have to bump over the lip and if you hit it just right it could "trip" the load and a ton of milk would go flying. I suggested they file the bottom of the new ramp lip instead of the top. This caused the ramp to meet the dock flat and loading was much smoother. I figured out a lot of little problems like that along the way and they were adapted for the most part. I even used a simple method of holding the 36 cases together while transporting them. Before that, they were free to just fall over, which they did a lot.

By the time we switched to semis and long trailers, we were delivering milk by the pallet of 36 cases of half gallon milk cartons. With 20 pallets, we would max out at 80,000 pounds weight. We had hand transporters to move the milk. We would bring it out on a tailgate and lower the pallet as soon as it cleared the truck bed and before it went off the edge. This was a precision move that had to be learned over time. Adding to this handicap was the fact that the early tailgates weren't up to the job. I had eight episodes where the tailgate "hinges" would break and a ton of milk, the transporter, and myself would fall to the ground. Luckily, I was never hurt but I spilled a lot of milk.

I've talked to people, later on in life, who were always amazed that I loved my job, while some of them hated their job and only did it for the money. In my opinion, liking what you do and striving to be the best at it is worth more than a better paying job that you don't enjoy. At the end of the day, I always felt I did a good job, even if I wasn't appreciated by the boss, and sometimes I wasn't. I worked for 24 years in a company where the boss later seemed to dislike me, for no reason that I could see. In 24 years, I took about two days sick leave and always showed up for work on time. No customers ever complained about me. I couldn't figure it out until about year 22. Another employee in another department was telling stories about me for years and I finally figured it out. The boss called me into his office one day and said he heard I was going to the union with a complaint. At that moment I realized who he heard that from. I confronted the boss with this information and set him straight. I talked to the other employee out on the job, and he told me he thought I should go to the union about a complaint from the boss against me. I replied, "You're probably right," although I had no intention of doing that. The next week the other employee was fired, and his job eliminated. I don't think he was fired because of me, but the fact he wasn't offered any other job is telling. I liked my job enough to overlook the pressure of indifference from the boss, for 22 years. After the other employee left, I noticed the boss asking my advice on things like I was the honorable employee I was. He finally noticed that I was knowledgeable about the whole operation, having been there longer than anyone else except him. He asked me one time why, if I didn't like it there, why I didn't leave. I tried to explain to him that, first, I had as much right to work there as he did, and second, I did like my job, despite his opinion. We didn't become close friends, but his attitude about me certainly changed.

Lost Child Found

Part 7: 1978, The Busy Years

My Uncle John invited me to attend a dance club where he was the president. I was reluctant because I was so busy at home, raising three girls, fixing meals, washing clothes, maintaining the house and the car, and generally being a good parent. He finally talked me into coming to at least one dance. There were married couples and singles of all ages, and it was good to get out of the house. I remember my first dance with a lady named Jane. Her first words to me were, "You're single, aren't you?" It kind of scared me, but we got along well. She asked what I did for a living, and I replied, "I'm a truck driver." She didn't think much of that, but it didn't end the conversation. Then she asked if I had kids. I explained I was a single parent, with three daughters, the youngest being seven. She replied: "You have what?" She had two boys, who were a little older and on their own.

Jane – Sperry Family Collection

It finally came time to sign up for the next session, and Jane discovered her partner wasn't signing up, and she couldn't, without a partner. At this point I asked if I could call her sometime and was she in the phone book? She replied she was but thought I should write down her phone number. I thought, "Yes, she's interested!"

Eventually I married Jane. Soon after I took a new job with a company that was starting up and was going to operate very much like the dairy where I had worked for 24 years. I was the number-two driver to be hired, the first being a relative of the new general manager. In the first year the new boss asked me to be on a committee to improve production in the company. Soon I was the committee chairman and went on to make more than 200 suggestions to improve the company. I was soon offered a place in management but was disappointed to watch him hire other people.

We drove brand-new Kenworth tractors that were gorgeous. They were painted red with chrome everywhere and were well equipped with gauges for everything and even an AM-FM radio AND a two way "CB" radio to talk to other drivers. All this before iPhones were even thought of.

About three weeks after finally opening, Sunnyside Farms burned down. A welder was doing the final touches on a machine, slipped and dropped the torch. It ignited a live hydraulic line and the hydraulic fluid blazed out of control, eventually setting the wooden roof on fire and completely burned everything. This put everybody out of work for the two years it took to rebuild. At my suggestion, when they rebuilt, they went from loading the trucks one stack of milk at a time, to having the milk on wheeled racks holding six stacks, which sped up loading at the plant and unloading at the stores. At the plant they went from two loading doors to eight and each truck could be loaded much faster.

Fire at Sunnyside Farms - Sperry Family Collection

During the two years off, I worked as a mechanic for several shops, almost becoming a journeyman mechanic, which took 6 months at that time. One of the best places I worked at was Orinda Shell, in Orinda. They had eight mechanics working six days a week. As I had truck experience, I became the tow-truck operator when needed. I applied for the job by mail and when I didn't hear back, I decided to drop in. The owner hadn't seen my application, so he invited me in for an interview. Then he asked when I could start. I replied, "Anytime." He said, "How about right now." I said I didn't have my tools with me. He replied, "Use mine." So, I started immediately. That's how busy the place was. He gave me the top work order off a tall stack of them and it turned out to be a Peugeot. I had never been close to one before, let alone worked on them. It wouldn't run and the boss said, "What will you do." I told him I would do a tune-up on it and see if that helped. That satisfied him and I went to work.

Another place I worked briefly was a garage in the Tenderloin district in San Francisco. It was owned by a neighbor. It was surrounded by one-way streets with no good place to park. I agreed to work there if I could park in his basement. That was agreeable and I started work. Every day I would have to drive around the place on the one-way streets to reach his driveway. At every corner there were prostitutes and beautifully dressed girls that looked like models. Bob informed me that "some of them were *really* women". Many were men in drag, and some were gorgeous. I worked on just about anything but tried to concentrate on Volkswagens. At the same time, I was fixing and building cars at home in the garage. I didn't need a chain hoist with a VW so I concentrated on them. One car I built contained body parts from three cars. When it was done, I spent two weekends painting it Corvette yellow. It was a $1,000 paint job on a $100 car. It was fun though.

I also drove "Eddie's truck". This was a three axle 1976 Freightliner cab-over with a comfortable 3/4 size sleeper unit. I was sub-leased to a place in Oakland dba (doing business as) "Keep on Trucking". Basically, we hauled anything that would fit on a 40-foot flatbed trailer. The truck had a 400 Cummins engine turned up to 450 hp on the dynamometer measured at the drive wheels. It probably was making 500 hp at the flywheel. It had a 13-speed transmission and was geared to go 100 mph. I'm sure it would do that as I tested it one night in the middle of Nevada. They were having an "independent truckers strike" and it was getting dangerous out on the road. People had windshields broken while they were driving and one driver was shot in Ogden, UT.

Eddie's Truck - Sperry Family Collection

Heading out of Wells, Nevada one night, I decided I would run with two other trucks for a little more protection. They were Peterbilt tractors with no trailers and as we gathered speed, I kept up with them until we were doing 90 mph. At this point, I decided I didn't want to drive this fast as I had a full load on the trailer. The truck was willing, but I wasn't.

While driving Eddie's truck, I was licensed for eleven western states. With a sleeper on the truck, I drove cross country and rested in the sleeper. No commute to work. Wake up and go, sometimes for 15 hours. I had to keep multiple logbooks in case I was stopped by the Highway Patrol. I could work 90 hours a week because of the sleeper, not all of it entirely legal ... but entirely safe. If I got tired I pulled over and slept. In this way I could drive 120,000 miles a year. As a result, I probably have 2.5 million miles in 18-wheelers alone (and close to that in cars), all in 48 years driving 18-wheelers with no accidents. After 23 years of retirement, I am sure the total is close to 4 million miles. I still drive very focused on what I'm doing so that sometimes I can't carry on a conversation because I'm too busy concentrating on drivers around me and conditions ahead. I absolutely concentrate on my driving. Many times, I have been able to drive through a possible accident just because I was paying attention. Now with the distraction of cell phones and infotainment systems on cars, and other distractions, it gets harder all the time.

With a 13-speed Road Ranger transmission, the shift pattern is to start in first gear, shift through five gears, and pull up a pre-select lever to go into high range. As you shift into sixth gear the transmission automatically shifts into high range. In sixth gear position, there is also a high and low range. This time, operated by a small lever on the gear shift knob. As you go through the top eight gears, you use that little lever quite a bit.

When they load a truck, the weight has to be placed properly, so you don't overload any axle. Sometimes you have to move the fifth wheel to change where the weight ends up on the tractor. The front axle normally can carry

12,000 pounds. The tractors dual drive axles can handle 34,000 pounds and the dual axle trailer can take 34,000 pounds for a total of 80,000 pounds on the whole 18-wheel truck. When you go through a proper CHP scale in California, they measure each set of axles and if you are overweight, on a set of axles, you have to move the load before continuing. You also get fined. This can be a problem if you're hauling a coil of steel, laying on its side on a pallet. Usually, you would use a forklift to move it. Out on the road you might not have that option. You have to figure out a way to move it by yourself. One way is to drop the trailer and fasten a chain on one side of the trailer, loop it around one side of the pallet and attach the chain to the tractor. Now you back up and pull the pallet forward or back to wherever it is legal and then chain everything back down again.

On one trip through Nevada, I had to move six bundles of "rebar" (reinforcement steel rod) one foot forward on the trailer. On the Utah-Nevada border, Utah will weigh you on the way out of their state and fine you $15 for an overweight. Nevada has no permanent scale, but you better get legal before entering California. The rebar was 45 feet long and hanging over each end of the trailer. Normally you would lift them with a chain hoist and move the 4-by-4 it is sitting on. On the road I found I could back up against a concrete freeway overpass in the middle of the night and move one bundle at a time by backing up. This placed the weight where it is legal and I passed through the next scale in California, OK.

I always tried to fill the fuel tanks before entering California, because the fuel was cheaper, with less taxes than in California. Eddie's truck had two 125-gallon fuel tanks, so I could go about 1000 miles in between fueling.

If I drove 55 mph, I could get 4.5 mpg. If I went 70 mph, I got 4.2 mpg. So, I drove 70 mph, where I could get away with it, as I was paid by the trip, and the faster I could go, the more money I made. It was very safe to do so and didn't stress the engine or the truck at all. The 11.00-22.5 radial Michelin tires on the truck were the best tires available and were in good condition.

On one trip, I was in Verdi, Nevada, unloading the load. As the forklift driver started to pick up a pallet, I was standing on the bed of the trailer, when suddenly the whole truck moved. I immediately thought the parking brake failed and rushed towards the cab. The movement stopped, and we both wondered what happened. I didn't figure it out until the next day. My next load was bound for Los Angeles, and I was highballing down Interstate 5, at my usual 70 mph, when I noticed a parked semi, off the road in front of me. It looked like part of his load had fallen off the truck. I soon discovered why. The pavement in front of me dropped about a foot, and I was briefly airborne. I definitely tested the limits of the air seat. Luckily my load didn't come off the truck, and no damage was done, and I continued my trip to L.A. The cause of all this turned out to be an earthquake in Chowchilla, California, the night before. We felt it, on the other side of the Sierra's, in Verdi, Nevada.

There are truck stops all over the place that are set up especially for long-distance truckers. The pumps are easy to drive up to, and the prices are usually competitive. They are easy to get into and easy to get out of. You're talking about a 65-foot-long vehicle, so the more room, the better it is. They usually have restaurants, and some have special sections just for truck drivers. Some have shower facilities that a driver can use if they buy fuel. A free three-minute phone call to anywhere in the United States is sometimes offered if you buy at least 100 gallons of fuel. That's easy to do as a lot of trucks have twin 125-gallon tanks, or more. With 250 gallons of fuel on board, I could go 1,000 miles between fuel stops. That was based on getting 4.2 miles per gallon at 70 mph with a full load of 80,000 pounds. I was licensed to drive in eleven western states and always fueled up in Nevada or Oregon, before entering California. The fuel is cheaper, mostly because of higher taxes in California.

After fueling and eating, a driver is free to park for the night and crawl into their "sleepers" and rest. Sometimes there can be over 100 trucks parked for the night, in a designated parking lot just for trucks. During the winter, it is common practice to leave the truck engines running, as they can be hard to start the next morning, if it's below freezing. It also keeps the driver warmer in the sleeper. My truck had three heaters, just for that purpose. It also had an external heater on the engine that would allow you to keep the engine block warm if you shut it down. It was thermostatically controlled, and a gasoline fired heater would start up, along with a water pump, and circulate warm water through the block, to keep it warm. I used it one night, and discovered it was not good if you were in the sleeper. It was too noisy when it started, periodically. It was better to lay there and listen to the diesel engine idle all night. You eventually got used to it. At least it's a steady noise. I usually put on a "winter front" if it was really cold. This is a cover for the radiator to allow just enough air to come through, to cool the engine, but not enough to cool the coolant too much. They were effective to zero degrees for me. Diesel engines use very little fuel while idling so it was the best way to go, if it was freezing.

Lost Child Found

On one trip through Nevada, I was in the middle of passing a "twin forty" (a truck hauling two forty-foot trailers), when the Honda Civic in front of me suddenly slowed, apparently to make a U-turn out in the middle of the desert. He hadn't signaled and was oblivious of anyone else on the road. It was completely unexpected, as we were 100 miles in any direction of even the smallest town. All I could do was hit the air horn and get as close to the "twin forty" as I could, half expecting to lose my right sideview mirror. I managed to avoid hitting anything, although I was probably a few inches from both of them. I later talked to the driver of the "twin forty" when we both stopped in Wendover for a bite to eat. He looked back when I honked and couldn't see any daylight between us. It was close. You see "twin forties" in places like Nevada, which is wide open country with hundreds of miles between anything. They also run "triples" in Nevada, a truck with three shorter trailers. They have to be the most unsafe rig on the road. I've seen too many of them, sitting on the side of the road, with the third trailer laying on its side. The third trailer tends to weave as they drive along. It doesn't take much to have them overturn.

The first time I drove over Donner pass at night, the snow was plowed beside the road, and it was higher than the semi van trailers that are limited to be thirteen feet six inches high. It was like driving through a curving tunnel, with no roof. The headlights lit up the clean snow and it sparkled like diamonds. When I reached Verdi, Nevada, on the other side of the pass, I pulled into a truck stop there, and encountered over 100 trucks parked for the night with their engines running. The ground and the trucks were covered with snow. Their exhaust rose into the fog and made for a surreal scene.

At rare times I encountered a prostitute roaming the area. They seemed to prefer "rest stops" along the freeways, so I usually stayed at real truck stops. I had one knock on the door, one night, asking for a "date". I told her, "Let me check with my wife." That got rid of her. Occasionally, I would hear people on the "CB" radio advertising something for sale. Sometimes legal stuff, and sometimes not. I was offered a fairly new fifty-foot-long canvas tarp, to cover a load. It was much better than the "throw away" blue tarp I was using. The price was right, so I bought it on the spot. I've been offered "reds" on the CB. Apparently, it's a drug to help you stay awake so you can drive illegal hours. Each state decides how long to allow a driver to operate. California allows 12 hours, while the rest of the western states allow 10 hours. You must keep a detailed logbook that should be kept up-to-date, showing the hours you drove and eventually turned in to your employer. At any time, a highway patrolman can request a look at your logbook. If it isn't up to date, you can be fined. They will allow a little give, because with the long distances between towns in the west, you could easily find yourself at hour ten in the middle of nowhere, with no safe place to pull over. I usually tried to make Winnemucca, Nevada, before pulling in to rest. It's 400 miles across Nevada, with only about three towns along the way. It's even worse on Highway six. There's only one town out there.

Sometimes I would end up in Northern Utah, and would go through Snowville, Utah, on my way back to California. I would drive 200 miles of two-lane road to intersect with Highway 80 at Wells, Nevada. It was a long lonely road, with nothing out there, except one restaurant that served very good food. The freight trains stopped there and that's what kept them in business. One time I turned onto the road at Snowville, and drove over a hill, to discover the road wasn't plowed, past the hill. I had nowhere to turn a big rig around, and so drove the 200 miles to Wells, on about a foot of unplowed snow. All I could do was crowd the middle of the road and hope I didn't slide off. I met one person, in a pickup, about 100 miles out. I had to hog the road as we passed, but I think he understood. If he slid off the road, I could pull him back on. If I slid off, I was going to be there a while.

I became a master of a now lost art. Before computers on vehicles, you could use the Jake Brake (Jacobs Engine Brake), as an aid in shifting. The Jacobs Engine Brake turns a switchable amount of cylinders in the engine to act as an air compressor, holding you back while going down a hill without using the service brakes. The RPM limit is usually 2100 RPM even in the newer engines. If you were in the right gear, you could switch "the Jake" to three settings, two cylinders, four cylinders, or six cylinders, and travel the forty miles of downhill on west bound Highway 80 over Donner Summit without touching the service brakes, with a full 80,000-pound load.

Going up or down through the gears you try for the fastest shift possible, so you don't lose road speed while shifting. Especially, going up a hill from a dead stop can be a challenge as you're losing speed while you're shifting, and a diesel engine only has 300 RPM to work with. The older trucks had a power range from 1800 to 2100 RPM. The newer ones were 1500 to 1800. Starting out, you ease out the clutch with the engine idling and run the engine up to its maximum RPM in first gear, ease off the throttle enough to get into neutral and then use "the Jake" to bring the RPMs down quickly and, at the right moment, ease the transmission into the next higher gear. You just use the clutch to get going in first gear, and never touch it again. If you're going up a hill and losing speed, and need to shift to the next lower gear, you wait for the minimum RPM and ease it into neutral and bring the RPMs up to the maximum speed and ease it into the next lower gear. In this way I was always able to get at least 100,000 miles on a clutch, the brakes, and the tires, if they were radials.

Heavy duty trucks are made to be repaired and run a long time. Some engines are built to go 600,000 miles before an in-frame overhaul is done. Frames are warranted for 500,000 miles and usually last for the life of the truck. It's not unusual to see many hundreds of thousands of miles on a heavy-duty truck.

I drove really old trucks that had a "five" and a "three" in them. That is a five-speed transmission main box with a three-speed Browny (Brownlite) transmission behind the main box. In shifting these you only used the clutch to get started. From then you shifted, bringing engine speed up or down, to match road speed and then it would shift smoothly. If you tried to use the clutch, it just wouldn't work. In the more modern transmissions, you would go through a "low range" pattern and then go into "high range" sometimes with a different shift pattern. You might have a 5-speed, 7-speed, 8-speed, 9-speed, 10speed, 13-speed, or even a 4-and-4 transmission. The shift patterns can be anything. A 10-speed might have a close ratio transmission where the last two gears are in a different place than the "normal" 10 speed. You have to go by the illustration on the gear shift knob to know what you have. To get a faster shift it was common to use the "Jake brake" to make RPMs fall quicker and get a faster shift. "The Jake" won't work with the clutch in. It takes a lot of practice to make this work smoothly, but once you get in the rhythm of it, it is a joy to behold. Newer trucks with computer-controlled engines won't let you do this. When you take your foot out of the gas, the engine RPMs hesitate for a couple of seconds before "the Jake" works and by then you have lost road speed and it spoils a quick shift. When I got my first "computer-engined" truck in 1995 I had this problem. I complained and they sent me to Freightliner to check it out. First, they had me run it on the dynamometer to check horsepower output and then checked the computer readout. Alas, it was up to specifications and couldn't be changed. I talked with a Cummins engine tech rep that was there and explained the difficulty of operating the Jake brake during shifting. He didn't understand how that could work, because "the Jake" doesn't work if the clutch is in. When I explained I didn't use the clutch past first gear, he was amazed. The Freightliner shop foreman told him a lot of "old timer" truck drivers used this method. The rep was a younger guy and had never heard of that.

When diesels first came out, they were limited in horsepower and would smoke easily if you "put your foot in it", which you had to do on a long hill. Soon, someone invented the turbo charger, a device that boosted inlet air pressure that mixed with more fuel and created more horsepower. In trucks it was found that the turbo broke up the smoke particles in the exhaust until they weren't so noticeable. For the first few years, they were known as "smog" turbos until they refined the engines to make more power without smoking. As late as 1970, some diesels were complicated to start, especially in cold weather. The procedure began with turning on the "glow" plug. This device warmed the air in the intake manifold. Next you would unlock a little pump handle and pump-up fuel pressure until it showed 100 psi on a small gauge. After locking the handle, you would pull out the compression release, a handle in the dash that pulled out about a foot and would open exhaust valves in the engine. Now you were ready to hit the starter. The "glow" plug would be warmed enough, the fuel pressure was "primed", and the compression was released to make it easier on the starter to turn the engine over. As you pressed the starter, you pressed the "ether" button (with your third hand) to help the engine ignite the first time, at the same time pushing the compression handle back into the dash. If everything went well, the engine would start with a cloud of black smoke. Then you warm it up for about 15 minutes. On the last diesel truck I drove, you could turn the starter with the key, like a modern car and the engine would start with less smoke than a lit cigarette, even after sitting for a couple of weeks.

I had a 1948 Kenworth "conventional" cab truck for a while. "Conventional" means there's a long hood out in front of you. If I stood in front of it, the top of the hood was over my head, and I was six feet tall at the time. Over the years, I lost two inches of height. I could lose sight of a car in front of me if they were too close. This happened a couple of times on the freeway when a car cut in front of me. Time for the air horn, although you only used it if you had to. Some people react by slamming on the brakes. A car turned left into one of the front wheels one time. It was night and even with all the lights a semi has they apparently didn't see me. The wheel shook violently, and I couldn't hold the steering wheel and we were on an overpass at the time, and I was looking down at the ground and railroad tracks far below. I managed to stop and got out to attend to the damaged car, which I saw in the side-view mirror in the act of spinning around. As a Highway Patrolman appeared, I told him what happened, but the car apparently took off. We inspected the truck's right front wheel and found paint from a blue car on the lug nuts. That was the extent of the damage to the truck, and we went on our way. The people in the car must have been high on something.

Eventually, Sunnyside Dairy reopened, and I was assigned to the "Tahoe" run. I would leave Vallejo at 3:00 am and drive up either Highway 50 or 80 to North or South Lake Tahoe. In the winter I would put six sets of chains on and off to make the trip. I got it down to about 15 minutes on and quicker off. Trucks are easier in a way than cars because you can get to the wheels without fenders in the way. There are more chains, and they are heavy, but you have more room to work with. On one trip up highway 50, I encountered a snowstorm that became a whiteout. I knew there were trees out there, but I couldn't see them for the snow falling. I could see the markers on the sides of the road that are put there for the snowplow drivers. I just centered myself between them and decided to see how far I could go. With six sets of chains and a load of 80,000 pounds not much could stop me unless I hit solid ice. I decided to just keep going. When I came down the other side of Echo Summit the road was closed and the chain control guy had to move barriers for me to get by. He asked me, "Where the h - - - did you come from?" I told him I had been up on the mountain for a good three hours. No one had any idea I was up there. At the store I walked in front of the truck, and you could see where I had been pushing snow with the front bumper of the Kenworth, which was about 18 inches off the ground. I should have billed "Caltrans" for plowing snow.

After doing this run for a couple years, I decided I couldn't do it anymore. Fifteen hours a day for three days a week might sound good, but it was wearing me down. They came up with a new way of paying overtime along the way. They called it a "rolling forty". You had to accumulate forty hours before overtime was paid. They also changed the overtime pay from "double time", to "time and a half". That killed a lot of overtime pay for me. I asked for the hours to be changed and middle management refused to do it. So, I gave him my notice and two weeks later I was gone. No one else would do those hours either, so they had to change them anyway. A couple of days before I left, the Big Boss approached me, after finally hearing I was leaving, and asked me to come see him. I never did, as I was done with that company. The following Christmas I was pleasantly surprised to receive my usual Christmas bonus. That was nice of them. They didn't have to do that, although I earned it.

My stepson Bill talked me into applying for a job with East Bay Water a couple of years before. I finally did apply, more to please him than anything else. I arrived for the written exam at a large building to find that 350 people applied for the one truck driving job. Some even drove a truck, but a lot were just trying to get a good job.

When I drove into Oakland to be tested in actually driving one of their trucks, I was still driving Eddie's truck for a living. I wish to this day I drove his Freightliner to the appointment, instead of our VW. It would be instant reputation. They had me inspect the small semi-truck before driving, with the company person along, to see how I did. I found a couple things on the truck that needed attention and that seemed to impress the inspector. When I drove, I further impressed him. I finally told him I drove for 31 years and knew what I was doing.

It took two years before I was finally chosen for the final interview with the Superintendent where I would work. They eventually hired me, and the new boss informed me they had a brand-new truck for me to drive. When I replied, "That's all I require," he laughed and told me I would do well there. This all fell into place soon after I quit the dairy job. I ended up working 16 years for East Bay Water, before I finally turned 65 and retired. I held out for "Heavy Truck Driver" as I knew I was qualified and it paid more. It turned out to be the best choice. "HTDs" were always chosen for working overtime jobs on water main breaks, usually in the middle of the night. We were also considered eligible to drive heavy equipment, so I got to drive bulldozers, backhoes, loaders, cranes and whatever else needed an operator. It was the best job, with the best people I ever worked with. When I retired, everyone was surprised because they didn't know I was that old.

When I was finally hired, they soon started changing from light weight trucks with Cat V-8s and automatic transmissions, to heavy duty Freightliners with manual transmissions. To their surprise, not many drivers were familiar with manuals. They promoted laborers and plumbers to drive their dump trucks and very few drove a stick shift truck. They had another driver and myself attempt to train people how to drive these much heavier duty trucks. We were given time off our regular jobs and a hat that said "Coach" on it. We were successful with most of the drivers, and today most of the fleet is heavy duty. The heavy equipment was improved also. They use John Deere and Volvo heavy equipment for most of their work now.

I started in North Yard, in Richmond. They have four yards, North, East, South, and Central, and they all concentrate on fixing leaks and installing new services and generally maintaining the hundreds of miles of mainline pipe that East Bay Water owns.

Soon they started a new division to do nothing but install new water mains. They called it Pipeline Construction Division, PCD, and I retired from that division. We streamlined how water mains are installed and it became a very important division, as a lot of the pipes in the ground are over a hundred years old and as they wear out PCD replaces them. Usually, I drove my own assigned 10-wheel dump truck, but would be called on to operate heavy equipment when needed. I think my favorite was a combination pipe hauler and crane. You sat in the middle of this machine and loaded a forty-foot pipe on each side. Then you drive it where the pipe can be lowered into the trench. Out go the outriggers for stabilization and the crane is then used to pick up the pipes and swing them around and lower them into the trench, all directed from a rigger, outside the machine. Everything is done by hand signals because sitting inside the machine you can't see much. You just watch the hand signals and operate about four or five levers to move the pipe. Sometimes you are raising the boom, lowering the steel cable, and swinging the boom, all at the same time. Sometimes an elbow comes in handy. I enjoyed running this machine and getting good at it. I also operated a backhoe, occasionally, but would not call myself proficient in it. That takes years of experience. I never broke anything, but I was very slow. We had operators who could, while digging a trench, sense something in the ground without breaking it. Sewer pipe is hard not to break, as it is made with very breakable terra cotta. They could somehow sense that and when it was dug up by hand there would not be a scratch on it. Amazing.

Along the way, East Bay Water bought some transfer trucks. That is a dump truck with a dump trailer. The dump body in the trailer is moved into the dump body on the truck, using a motor in the dump body. They were also called "slam-bangs" for the noise they make. I learned how to back these up to a backhoe, sometimes having to end up in a different "lane". When you dump, you disconnect the trailer and dump your load, then return and line up the truck on the trailer and "transfer" the trailer body into the truck dump bed. After you return the trailer dump body to the trailer, you move forward and reconnect the truck to the trailer. They also had a couple long semi dump trailers. They could be tricky, though. When dumping, if the load "sticks" in the front of the trailer, a slight breeze can knock you over. Sometimes that drags the whole truck with it and the whole rig ends up on its side.

Slam Bang - Sperry Family Collection

Section Two:

Finding My Roots

and Much More

Lost Child Found

Part 1: 2005, Following the Paper Trail

About 2005, I received a 23andMe DNA kit, for Christmas. At an early age, I was told my birth father was full-blooded Czechoslovakian. It was, therefore, a great surprise when no Czech showed up in my DNA. I then got another DNA test kit from Ancestry to check and when it was run, it was very close to the 23andMe DNA test. It did say about 22% western Europe, but I was looking for 50% from my full blood father. That stirred my curiosity to find my ethnicity and, by this time, what my birth parents died of. So, I started a thirteen-year search for my beginnings.

I started with what I had, an information sheet that came with me from the "Native Daughters Central Committee on Homeless Children". It listed a name, age, religion, and place of birth of my birth parents, along with occupation and a short description of them.

I looked up my "father", Robert Allen, and discovered a couple of pages of Robert Allen's in the 1935 San Francisco phone book. I also looked in a book of Civil Engineers in California during the period he should have been there. After comparing many names, it was a dead end. With such a common name, I was forced to quit.

My birth-mother's name was given as Virginia McMeans along with a mention of the names Evelyn and Jean. The name on my first Birth Certificate was Robert McMeans with my parents being Jean McMeans and Robert Allen.

The info sheet also said my father was a Civil Engineer working as a Surveyor, a pretty good job during the height of the Depression. It told where he worked and his job, but these were censored out. It gave his birthplace as

Czechoslovakia. My birth-mother was going to college to be a nurse or teacher. She was listed as born in California. She met my father while visiting her brother in .... My birth-father worked as a surveyor on the .... He was listed as a Civil Engineer with education of Junior College - intelligent man, as they wrote it.

There was mention of Virginia's mother having a breakdown, but that it wouldn't affect the baby.

The State of California, which has taken over all adoption records from the "Daughters of the Golden West", sent me a report that states my birth-mother's father was a Postmaster. This was new information from my first "background information request".

With McMeans to go on I started with my "mother's" name. I eventually found a Virginia McMeans working as a servant in San Francisco, in the 1940 census. Her usual job was listed as nurse. This was still the depression until World War 2 broke out. I also found a Virginia McMeans in the 1940 census in Rogersville, Alabama. Are they the same person? They are the same age, have a medical background and are the only Virginia McMeans to be found. Under the "Procedural History of 1940 Census of population and housing" rules, page 31, I found -- "General Instructions: Usual place of residence". This instruction is to count all persons including persons who were temporarily absent. So, she could very well have been registered in California where she was living, and in Alabama where she is temporarily absent. A Genealogy expert has told me that happens all the time.

During this time, I contacted the State of California, which had taken over the records of the Native Daughters Adoption information. They are really tight about adoption information, even seventy years after the fact.

The first correspondence showed the same thing as my information sheet. The second correspondence, a couple of years later, showed a little more. It showed my father working nearby as a "Highway" surveyor. That fact turned out to be an important clue. It also showed the occupation of my birth-mother's father as being a Postmaster. This turned out to be important, too.

I was using the search engine that comes with Ancestry and found only one Virginia McMeans. There was no Evelyn or Jean McMeans listed so I went with Virginia. If she was born in California, there was no record, but there was a wealth of information about a Virginia McMeans born in Rogersville, Alabama, across the Tennessee River from Wheeler Dam Village. She was the right age, the right general description, and planned to be a nurse at the right time, and I found evidence of a Virginia McMeans in San Francisco, five years after I was born. She then appears in Alabama working as a receptionist for a doctor in Florence; this is 37 miles from Rogersville. About this time the war started, and Virginia enrolled in Vanderbilt University School of Nursing in Nashville, Tennessee, to become an Army Nurse.

At about the same time the doctor she worked for in Florence, Alabama, went to Vanderbilt University and was in the Army as a Major during the war.

She served until the war was over and then worked as a stewardess for Seaboard and Western Airlines which flew between Europe and New York City. She was #29 stewardess hired. At that time a stewardess had to be a RN. This airline later became FedEx. She flew to Casa Blanca, Munich, Berlin and other exotic places before finally working at Presbyterian Hospital in New York City. She finally married a Doctor from Florence,

Alabama who, twenty years earlier, had gone to Vanderbilt College at the same time Virginia had. I suspect he was also the doctor she was a receptionist for in 1940. In the 1940 census, it shows her home address on a street that crosses a street were the doctor practiced. In researching Virginia, I discovered a younger sister by the name of Ruby. She had a daughter, Anne. By 2005 Anne has her DNA taken and is in Ancestry. I contacted her and she answered a lot of my questions and cleared up some of the mystery. I asked her if Virginia ever had a nickname, and she answered, in her slight Alabama accent, "Aunt Ginny never had a nickname." I finally pointed out that if she said "Ginny" in California, everyone would assume your name was Jean. In her soft Alabama accent, Ginny sounded like "Jeany". She said of Virginia marrying the doctor, that she loved him forever and finally they were married.

About this time the State of California informed me my birth-mother's father was a Postmaster. Soon after, the Post Office came out with a website, where you could enter a name or a place and it revealed that Virginia's father, Jester, was a Postmaster in Rogersville, Alabama.

In further correspondence with Anne, she related family memories of something happening in the family in the mid-thirties that no one would talk about.

My "family" is listed in Ancestry as being from the British Isles and Pacific Rim and is Christian/Protestant as on my info sheet. My 23andMe DNA shows English, Irish, and a small amount of Native American, where they mention Peru. I find a relative of Virginia's living in Tennessee which is another interesting fact to remember as I continue my search.

Virginia McMeans had an older brother which was mentioned in my info sheet.

Anne is very kind and helpful with me, up to a point, but she doesn't think Virginia could be my mother.

Everything matches, except the DNA. Anne and I should be first cousins with a huge amount of common DNA. There is none. I used six years investigating "Jean" McMeans, accumulating 88 pages of closely spaced information found in different places, using Ancestry's many search engines. There is no doubt in my mind that Virginia McMeans could have had a child in San Francisco in 1935. It just wasn't me.

23andMe logo – Courtesy of Wikimedia Commons

Part 2: 2011, Follow the DNA

FOLLOW THE DNA.

I have thousands of DNA relatives in Ancestry, none of them familiar to me. There are no McMeans mentioned and just a few Allen's well down the list. I checked out the Allen's and none are close to being the right age or in the right place or being a civil engineer or a nurse. I look for relatives who have an ancestor that might be who I am looking for. It is unlikely my parents would have a DNA test as they were around long before it was invented. They would be over 100 years old.

I am looking for ancestors that would be the right age and reasonably close to San Francisco. At this point I can't tell which parent they are. I am looking for people that would have been in their 20's or 30's when I was born.

I started by trying to find a" common ancestor" in my many DNA relatives. I found the name Waites is common on several DNA relative's family trees. They go back in time to before there was an America. They were here first and when the American Revolution came, they fought in it. They were also in all the rest of our wars. All the Waites in the military had grey eyes. I have grey eyes. Maybe I'm on to something. I'm definitely related to these guys but is it from my father's side or my mother's side? That's what I have to figure out. I have to find a common ancestor in my DNA relatives, search their family trees, that may not be accurate but they are recollections of my relatives and perhaps I can find someone in the right age group that could be my birth parents. This is tedious because many parents had up to 20 children, the farther back I go. When I find someone likely, Ancestry gives me the option of contacting their descendants through Ancestry. They don't have to answer me, and many don't.

One thing I learned quickly: when contacting people don't mention adoption right away. I may never hear from them again. Better to ease into it gradually. Of course, if I knew who my family was, things would move along much more smoothly.

In my list of DNA relatives, Ancestry lists the closest ones first and they measure the closeness in "centimorgans". The more centimorgans, the closer related they are. If I can pick up a thread in my closer DNA relatives, it makes my search easier. This would be much easier, because now I'm looking at names I recognize. The farther down the list I go, the more names get mixed up. Every time a woman marries, her last name changes. That's why maiden names are so important and used in Ancestry. My DNA relative may be a few names removed from who I am looking for.

In Ancestry, there is a search engine called "California Birth Index". In it I can enter a maiden name or a date of birth or the name of the child. Any two will trigger a search for the rest. The program will show the county where I was born and my gender. I do not find any McMeans. I do find several Waite maiden-names. Some had a child around the time I was born in San Francisco. Two are very close to the time I was born. Their married names are Watson and Poulson. I must check them out. I suspect I might have been switched at birth with another child. Because I was put up for adoption, the State has hidden my birth-mother's name, but I have my information sheet that came with me with the name McMeans as my birth-mother. I also obtained my original birth certificate with my name as Robert McMeans on it. This is identical to my second birth certificate except my name has changed to what my adopted parents named me. Could a Waite baby be mixed up with a McMeans baby at the hospital? The babies that were put up for adoption were housed in "cottages" in the Avenues in San Francisco. About 13 babies to a "cottage" with one nurse to care for them. It might be easy to get mixed up there, too.

Alice Waite Watson lives in San Francisco in 1935 and was born in 1899; a little old to be my birth-mother. She marries Lewis Watson, but I can't find a date. In the 1940 census, they are living in Redwood City, CA, south of San Francisco. The census says their residence in 1935 is San Francisco. Their child, Richard, is listed as 4 years old. Margaret Waite (misspelled Warte) 64 (an Ancestry user) lived with them. Richard goes to U.C. Berkeley in 1954 and also Stanford. Alice is a stenographer living on Jackson Street in San Francisco in 1933.

I have 45 pages of notes on Alice Waite. I must remember that Waite might be on my birth father's side. I have to check out both genders to figure it out.

Robert Poulson's mother's maiden name is Waite. He was born November 15, 1935 in San Francisco. He is 5 days younger than I. They lived in San Francisco in 1935. Another possible match, if I was switched. I have 14 pages of notes on them. I don't go as far with them, because I decide I don't want to disrupt people's lives at this point in time. They would have to investigate the same material I have and come to the same conclusion. If one had DNA related to Anne in Alabama that I talked to, that would explain everything and prove that Jean McMeans did have a baby in San Francisco in 1935. If her niece, Anne McMeans never had a DNA test done, none of this would have come up. That's part of the problem. As more people are tested, it will be easier to figure things out.

So, I'm thinking I might have been switched between a McMean baby and a Waite baby. If one or the other ever got DNA tested, they would discover they weren't DNA related to their mother. If I was DNA related to either of the Waite mothers, that would explain that. I am hesitant to approach either one as they have lived their whole lives believing this is really their mother. I don't want to upset that apple cart.

My first DNA relative is "R.S." (an Ancestry user) with 677 centimorgans (centiM) and is likely a first cousin. He is administrated by my third DNA relative, "psheehe" who with 304 centiM is likely a second cousin. She has a family tree with 4941 people in it. Keep in mind a person's child might have 3457 centiM with a grandchild having 2046, as a comparison.

"Psheehe" turns out to be Patty Sheehe, whose father is R.S. His mother is Margaret Bennett, born in California in 1903. We are DNA related. She's in the right age group to be my birth-mother. She is not, as it turns out, but you have to investigate her. Her mother is Ida May Waite and her father Elliot Waite is a" common" DNA relative, shared by a few other family groups.

I look at the union of Edward Bennett and Ida May Waite, who are DNA relatives. From them I come up with 23 people who are the right age.

Ida May married Edward Bennett whose child is Margaret. Now I look to see if Margaret has siblings. She does and one is the right age, so I check him out too. It turns out there are 2 siblings who are male, in the right age area and both are surveyors. Thinking back to my information paper my "father" was a surveyor. It's not the name on my "information" sheet but I am DNA related to these two men and they are the right age. They are both long dead and there's no DNA from them to check, but because of their relationship to Margaret, we are related. Neither had children, except for maybe me. So, there is no direct offspring to check DNA with. You can do a search on Ancestry and the census is a great place to look. They show both brothers working as surveyors in 1940 but one is working for the California Department of Roads. The other works elsewhere.

There is also Elmer Waite who is the right age and was living in California at the time I was born. He must be checked out. He marries Marjorie Renfrew and has a child who is listed in my DNA relative base and goes by "ktdid1946". We are probably second cousins.

Some I can eliminate but some are possible and will have to be investigated further. If you go to Ancestry and enter a family tree you can find a person of interest and click on their name. If you then click on "Profile" it will take you to a page with links to their "Life Story" or "Facts" and, finally, "Gallery" which will show pictures if any are available. From these you can get a wealth of information. There are also "Sources" on the "Facts" page such as different census, military records, and many more. The census is the most reliable and sometimes will show mistakes in the "Tree" such as an unreported child in the "Tree".

When I look through the hundreds of names that are possible parents, I look for what they were doing when I was born. If they're married with children in another state, they probably won't be my parent. If they are single, they get another look. Using the search engine in Ancestry will lead me to Newspaper articles, different census reports, military records, notices of marriage, death and others. When I searched myself, as a test, I found a newspaper article in the Oakland Tribune from 1957 that I didn't know about, describing a car race I won.

After determining which "Common Ancestor" DNA relatives are on my "father's" side, I can assume the rest are on my "mother's" side.

Adoption – Courtesy of Creative Commons NounProject.org

Part 3: 2018, The Payoff

In late February, 2018 a new DNA relative appeared on Ancestry. The post said the person was a first cousin or close family. The centimorgan's were 1682, which is the highest of any DNA relative on my list, by far.

On Friday, Feb.23, 2018 at 8:02 pm, I sent an email to Barrie:

> "Hi Barrie. So, my wife, Jane, and I live in Groveland, CA. in the foothills of the Sierra Nevada Mountains. Where do you live? We share an account on Ancestry, so it gets mixed up once in a while. It looks like our common ancestor might be LaRoe, Wheeler, Edwards, Pickering and more. Does that ring a bell?"

Barrie returns my email:

> "Pretty sure that Wheeler would be the only *connection*. I live in Canada now, but my mother, Evelyn Wheeler was born in Santa Rosa, CA. Her father was Robert Bruce Allen Wheeler. Her mother was Rose Hudoff Wheeler. My mother had two siblings, Doris and Vernon. Doris had only one natural child, Jean, who now lives in Sacramento. Vernon had several children by his first marriage. I believe they may have lived in Eureka. The only name on that side I can remember is Dolores, who was my mom's niece. She lived in Redding."

At this point, I take another look at annie78's tree, which showed Robert and Rose Wheeler with Doris and Vernon, but no Evelyn. In looking at Robert Wheeler's "Profile

Facts" I look at the "Source" column and find a 1940 census. In it is Robert and Rose with Vernon and Doris AND Virginia Evelyn Wheeler. Evelyn's birthday, October 27, 1916, is the same date as on my "info" page that came with me from the "Daughters Home". This strongly suggests Evelyn is my birth mother and Barrie is my half-sister. I never gave a thought to having siblings, maybe because I was raised an only child. Barrie doesn't know this yet and I must approach this news carefully or she might disappear, like others have on Ancestry. She asks my mother's maiden name and where I was born, and I intentionally ignore her questions and ask her others.

I correspond again, this time using our actual email addresses instead of going through Ancestry, where you can quit corresponding at any time:

> "Thanks so much for getting back to me so fast. Been busy today. You say Doris had one 'natural' child. I'm not sure what that means. What was your mother's married name? Do you have siblings? Does the name Haas mean anything to you? I grew up in Oakland, CA. We have two grandchildren that live in Santa Rosa. I would direct you to 'annie78' on Ancestry. Her Tree includes a lot of Wheeler's and is a mutual common DNA relative I believe. Do you have a Family Tree up yet? ttyl...Paul"

Barrie answers:

> "My father's name was Brower. So my mom was Evelyn Wheeler Brower. She was married again after a divorce from my father. My aunt Doris Smith adopted a son, Robert in 1941 and then became pregnant later with Jean. So, my cousin Robert would not have been related via

DNA, that was what I meant by one natural child, perhaps the wrong word. I have one brother, Bruce Brower who lives in Lakeport, CA. He has two daughters who live in Petaluma area (and 4 grandkids). My father had a brother who did not have any children so that is kind of a dead end. I do not yet have a membership in Ancestry so am not sure I can access that family tree for annie78. I guess I need to bite the bullet and try it out. My uncle Vern's kids' names may be Dolores, Patricia, and Robert and there were others. I cannot remember the family name they had. There was something that happened, so Vern was estranged from his kids. They ended up being raised by their maternal grandparents and took their name. I have only met Dolores once (she passed away about two years ago). Her family lives in the Redding area. Her married name was Carvalho, I think. Haas isn't a name I recall or see anywhere in my history. Here are a bunch of names in no particular order: Brower, Hopper, Allen, Hudoff, Deeths, Patterson, Wilcox, Troll, Knieb, Lownes. The Brower and Hoppers all settled in Potters Valley, near Ukiah. My great grandmother Elizabeth Lownes Hopper was born in Benicia in 1854 and then lived in Potters Valley. She lived to be 101 years old. The Wheeler's and Allen's were in Santa Rosa. All of the other names are further back in history. Perhaps you may see some of these names in your tree. Which one of you is related to the Wheelers. Sorry to be so long winded, but this is really a mystery!!! DNA at first cousin level should be somebody we both would know about, you would think."

Barrie hasn't made the connection yet, and I'm not answering her questions because I don't have a family tree and I don't know my birth mother's name or any of the other names. Wow, I also have a brother.

Two hours later Barrie emails again:

> "Just looked at annie78 on Ancestry and what I can see without getting the whole family tree is that she is related to the name Allen in 1840 which is the date I have for my great-great grandfather Allen. His daughter Alta Allen [Wheeler] was my great grandmother. She married George Wheeler. It doesn't seem to explain a first cousin relationship though. Do you know what your relationship is to annie78? By the way I live in Mississauga, a suburb of Toronto in Ontario. We are in Eastern Time Zone, three hours later than California."

I email Barrie back:

> "Thanks for the info. It's a mystery to me, too. Do I show up on your DNA stuff? I'm shown as P.S., which stands for Paul Sperry. Annie78 is another of my DNA relatives on that side. On the other side the name Waite shows up as the common ancestor. If you sign up for Ancestry you have access to other programs such as "Search" which is like Google search but more helpful. Does Native American show up in your ethnicity? It does on mine and in annie78. It shows Choctaw in Virginia in the 1700s. Does Bruce live in Lakeport, CA? I asked about Haas because they lived in Marin County but they're on the other side. Wheeler is the common DNA ancestor between you and annie78. They measure closeness by centimorgans

and DNA segments. There is a chart that shows where you might be and you are my closest DNA relative by far. Has Bruce had a DNA test? Or anybody else? The more the merrier."

Barrie answers very quickly:

> "Bruce lives in Lakeport, CA. and as far as I know he hasn't done the DNA test nor has anybody else in my immediate family. I only have one living first cousin as far as I know. Just to make sure, it is Paul Sperry that I am writing to and not Jane Sperry? How old are you? Where were you born? Where was your mother born? I do not have any Native American in my DNA report although family oral history hinted at that.
>
> "What is your relationship to annie78? Is she someone you have placed in your family tree? Do you know anything else about her? Age? Place of birth. Not sure how to put this but there is a possibility that I might have a half sister who would be in her late 70s or early 80s now. She would have been adopted and so might not show up looking at last names and traditional family tree information but would surface with DNA tests. Will likely sign up for Ancestry in order to take a good look at the other information they have on file. I can also enter the family tree information that I already know. Thanks for all the hints."

Wow. Now Barrie is starting to catch on. I write her back with a loaded question:

> "You are talking with Paul Sperry. Jane is my wife, and we share the Ancestry site. I'm not

sure how to put this either but might you have a half-brother instead of half-sister?"

Almost there. She writes back:

    ✉   "I suppose it might be a half-brother."

I reply:

    ✉   "I am 82, born in November, 1935 in San Francisco. Annie78 is the 5th DNA relative in my list, a 2nd or 3rd cousin. Looking at her tree, the Native American is on the other side from Wheeler. Surprisingly there are Allen's on both sides with Samuel Allen born 1770 marrying Malinda Harr, supposedly a Choctaw native American from Virginia."

Barrie writes back:

    ✉   "This may sound farfetched, and I apologize ahead of time if you find the suggestion offensive. Could there be a possibility that you were adopted?"

I reply, holding my breath:

    ✉   "I am hesitant to mention that I'm adopted as I have had people stop talking. I was adopted in San Francisco and grew up in Oakland."

Barrie has figured it out:

    ✉   "OMG. Well, this is getting more and more interesting by the moment. I have to tell you that my mother told me that she had a child out of wedlock who was adopted. That would have been in the late1930's. It was very upsetting to her to talk to me about it as she had kept it a secret for so long. She only told me when she was in her 70s or

80s. I did not write down when she had the child, but your dates and the location of birth make sense. She would have been 19 years old. I thought she told me it was a girl, but maybe I didn't remember it that well. This is totally boggling my mind. Do you know anything at all about your birth mother?"

I quickly answer:

> "This is exciting. All I have is an information sheet from the Native Sons and Daughters stating my mother's birthday as 27 October 1916. She was just 19. They have her name as Virginia McMeans. It says she had gone to Junior College and played violin. Her mother was German, and her father was German-Scotch-Irish."

Barrie:

> "I cannot believe this. Amazing. That is totally my MOTHER, well, also your mother. How awesome for you. Now you will be able to know more about her. Her birth name was Virginia Evelyn Wheeler (she never liked the name Virginia and always went by Evelyn). I will have to get together some photos of her to send to you. Unfortunately, she passed away in November 2011 at the age of 95. I think we are going to have a lot to talk about. I was going to attach a photo of my brother and me, but it is one of those days where nothing works. Please feel free to ask anything you might want to know about her. I have a ton of family history, but not very organized."

Lost Child Found

Bruce Brower, my half-brother and clone – Sperry Family Collection

Paul Sperry, Barrie Brower, and Bruce Brower newly found half siblings – Sperry Family Collection

What does it feel like to discover you have half siblings you never knew existed and you're 82?

It's magic.

I never even thought about siblings. It just never occurred to me. We meet and fit together like missing pieces of a puzzle. They knew about me, and they never hesitated accepting me. Our mother told them about me in her 80's. From then on, they referred to me as "The Lost Child". They say she was really upset when she talked about me. It seems she had feelings for me that lasted more than 80 years to the point she told my siblings about me. She certainly didn't have to do that. Her secret was well hidden for all that time.

Barrie is coming to Victoria, B.C. for a pre-planned visit with a girlfriend. I'm able to get the last seat on a flight going there and we arrange to meet. I don't know how I will react. I can get emotional watching the news and leak tears. As I approach the lobby of our hotel, I take a deep breath. I open the door and there is Barrie. She stands and we embrace like we've known each other forever. It's amazing. No tears, just joy. Later, Jane and I meet Bruce and his wife Paula, at the Train Museum in Sacramento. Before this I receive a picture and we resemble each other so much that I decide to test my three daughters. I send them Bruce's picture with no explanation. They all assume it is me and return greetings like "Looking good", and similar things.

We even dress alike and like our hands in our pockets – Sperry Family Collection

Barrie and Bruce accept me immediately. They recognize things about me that are common with our mother and even our grandfather. My sense of humor is like my grandfather's. The constant song going on in my subconscious is definitely like my mother. I notice we all have vertical lines on our ear lobes, crooked index fingers, and bad knees.

Bruce (L) and Paul (R) in their 40's long before they knew each other existed – Sperry Family Collection

Bruce and I share an amazing 2024 centiMs. That's as close as a grandchild. We turn out to be like clones. We share an interest and talent in anything with wheels. I've always worked on my own cars and even as an automotive mechanic at times. Bruce is very mechanical too. So is Barrie. She tore the engine down on her lawnmower and fixed it. It runs great now. Not bad for a woman trained as a Botanist. Bruce and I both had HO gauge model trains growing up and are still into it on a smaller scale. In our early 20's we both bought a BSA twin cylinder motorcycle. We also had '50 Ford pickups. We both raced cars and motorcycles. We both have an interest in photography. I

Lost Child Found

used to develop and print my own black and white photos when I was 10 years old. He worked as a photographer for Bechtel on the Alaskan Pipeline. As it turns out I learn photography runs in the family. A couple of grandfathers had photo shops back when photography was in its beginnings. I discover all the men in our family part their hair on the right side, myself included. We all have great bones and lousy cartilage. Barrie and I have artificial joints and Bruce now takes Hyaluronic Acid for his knees, just like I do. Bruce and I share a passion for vanilla ice cream. I find out our mother had a talent for playing stringed instruments and just about everything else. I've played guitar since I was 11 years old. The list goes on and on.

Vintage BSA Motorcycle Poster – Courtesy of Art.com

When Bruce worked on the Alaskan Pipeline, for Bechtel, we might have met. As a photographer he was everywhere taking pictures. I took a course called "Industrial Instrumentation" in hope of getting a job there working with the many valves required. If that didn't work, I could apply as a truck driver. It was not meant to be, as my wife at the time vetoed that idea. When we were younger, Bruce and I looked like twins. I sent an old picture of him to a friend of 40 years, and she swore it was me and I was just kidding her.

Now I know exactly where I came from. The western Europe part in my DNA is Germany. My grandmother was from Hanover. The rest is the usual English, Scotch Irish mixture most people have. The Wheelers started out in Knoxville, Tennessee, after arriving in Virginia from England. How I wish I knew that when Robby Robbins, from Tennessee, was my roommate in the Air Force.

My great-great grandfather, Jacob Wheeler, headed out to Oregon with his brother when he was 16. He homesteaded 640 acres in what is now East Portland, that is known as the Wheeler Addition. About 1848, he made a side trip to visit the California gold fields. He came back with $4,400 ($102,000 today), not bad for a young man in those days. He then improved on his land, got married along the way, and sent a lot of his fallen trees to San Francisco where they became pilings in the new harbor they were building. Eventually, he and his family ended up in Santa Rosa, California with $65,000 in cash, ($1,464,000 today) a fortune back then. The trip was made because of his wife's health. It turned into another lucrative time to be in a new place just starting out. He was very successful in Santa Rosa in dealing with selling and buying land there and developing it. He died in 1905 and so missed the San Francisco earthquake of 1906. It made a mess of Santa Rosa too and the governor declared that no more land could be sold in Santa Rosa because of the earthquake threat. This wiped out the family business overnight. Eventually, that all changed as Santa Rosa now is a thriving suburb of San Francisco.

Virginia Evelyn Wheeler at Stanford – Sperry Family Collection

Lost Child Found

I learned that my grandfather, who was a Postmaster, built a house in Santa Rosa just before the 1906 earthquake when the cripple walls failed. Eventually it was rebuilt to its original style and is still there in its original form. Here, our mother was born in 1916. It is in the historical part of Santa Rosa and just down the street from where Luther Burbank lived and did his work. He was friendly with our grandfather and would come up the creek and have coffee in the back yard. There are Luther Burbank trees in that back yard to this day.

Curiously, it is a couple of blocks from Wheeler Street.

Santa Rosa House - Sperry Family Collection

Lost Child Found

Bruce tells me the family always believed they were related to "Fighting" Joe Wheeler, famous for his action in the Civil War where he became a General for the South, after graduating from West Point. Later, after being a congressman from Alabama, the President asked for his service, this time for the Union Army. He became a General again and commanded the "Rough Riders" in Cuba and later fought in the Philippines. A picture shows him in Cuba with Theodore Roosevelt also in the picture.

Fighting Joe Wheeler (front) with Theodore Roosevelt (right) 1898 – Courtesy of WeAreTheMighty.com

Bruce remembers seeing a Confederate uniform in our grandfather's closet that was complete down to the shoes and sword and was said to be from Joe. Grandfather also looked like "fighting" Joe. They called him that after having 16 horses shot out from under him and being wounded three times, all in the Civil War. Joe is one of very few Confederate soldiers buried at Arlington National Cemetery. Joe also has a statue in the National Rotunda in the nation's capital, representing the State of Alabama. An early picture of him shows that he parts his hair on the right, just like Bruce and grandfather and I do.

*Fighting Joe Wheeler Statue at the US Capitol Rotunda –
Courtesy of Architect of the Capitol AOC.gov*

After the Civil War, Joe settled in northern Alabama and eventually began serving many terms as a congressman. The place he lived was named Wheeler, in his honor. Also, within 40 miles is Wheeler Dam and Village, on the Tennessee river. Nearby is Wheeler State Park and Wheeler Wildlife Refuge. Right in the middle of all this sits Rogersville, Alabama, where Jean McMeans was born. If Jean had shared a room with my birth mother in the maternity ward, she surely would have asked about the Wheeler name. This is just another coincidence in my long search for the truth. I probably will never know the answer to this question as all the actors are long gone.

Wheeler Memorial (1836-1906) – Courtesy of FindaGrave.com and Ron Williams

My birth mother wrote a long rambling 61-page journal that includes information on my birth-father. She mentions he was a surveyor working on what became State Highway 299 near Redding.

My "info" sheet tells of her meeting my birth father while visiting her brother's wife in————. He's working on the ——————————. Arcata and Redding-Alturas Highway fit exactly in those censured spaces. It says he's a Civil Engineer working as a surveyor. This also corresponds with my birth mother's journal. This corresponds with a Waite relative, "psheehe" or Patty Sheehe who is in the Family Tree #3 on my DNA Relatives list. Elliott Bennett was a 31-year-old civil engineer working as a surveyor for the California Department of Roads in Northern California in 1935.

In a journal I found under Ancestry Search, I found the "State of California Highways and Public Works" 1935 edition of some outstanding projects. The State built 6,700 miles of new highway that year. On page 11, it details some outstanding projects, among them the Redwood Highway in Sonoma County which runs right through Santa Rosa. It also mentions the Redding-Alturas lateral in Lassen and Modoc County. This runs through Redding. My birth mother's brother lived in Arcata at that time and my birth mother visited them and while there, met my birth father. The journal tells quite a bit about him, but no name.

In Ancestry the name Elliott Bennett is a DNA relative and in the 1940 census he is working for the California State Roads Department as a "chainman", a surveyor. He is the same age as the "information" sheet. Arcata is at the beginning of Highway 299. This is a picture of Elliott, taken in Wyoming on an unknown date where he looks like he might be on the job out in the countryside. He looks like I certainly could be related. He doesn't marry until in his 50's and has no known children, except maybe me.

Elliott Bennett in Wyoming – Courtesy of Patty Sheehe

As a surveyor, Elliott likely worked on Highway 80 when they built it. Highway 80 stretches the entire width of the

U.S. from San Francisco to Teaneck, New Jersey. My adopted Dad worked on Highway 80 at Donner Pass about the same time.

Elliott's mother is a Waite. The Waite's were in America before there was a United States. They fought in the Revolutionary war and every war since then. All the men in the military had grey eyes. I have grey eyes.

I talked to a DNA relative in San Bernardino who was his niece. She didn't know much about him because he was always away on a job somewhere. He was the right age, in the right job, in the right place, at the right time. We are DNA related. I think he was my birth father. Without further information, I can go no further, but everything seems to match.

Under 23andMe my DNA shows a small amount of Native American, from Peru. In family trees from my father's side, I find a Native American ancestor from 1700, in Virginia, who is from the Choctaw tribe. It is the only reference I find of an actual Native American ancestor. The Choctaw were marched to Oklahoma on what was later called "The Trail of Tears".

The name of my father on my info sheet is Robert Allen. My grandfather's name is Robert Bruce Allen Wheeler. It's likely my birth mother came up with that name as an easy one to remember without using the true name. I don't know where his place of birth came from. Czechoslovakia seems like an unlikely place to write in, and maybe that's the point. Everything else on the info sheet appears to match my birth parents. Just not their true names. The birth date for my birth-mother on the info sheet is exactly correct. I have over 90 pages of notes on Elliott Bennett. That's what it takes to try to find the truth.

In "Additional History" on the back of my information sheet, is a description of my birth-mother graduating from Junior College and plans to go on to be a nurse or teacher. She actually went to Stanford to be a doctor, and later switched to nurse's training as her parents couldn't afford the additional expense for her to become a doctor in the middle of the great depression. She had the grades to qualify her for doctor training. In later years, she became an 8th grade math teacher.

So, after 13 years of tedious searching I have found out who I am, where I came from, and made contact with my brother and sister. It was a long haul but well worth it. For others attempting to find your ancestry, especially if you're an adoptee, FOLLOW the DNA. The information may be there. You just have to recognize it and dig it out. With the internet the job can be done. There is endless information there. As others get their DNA tested it will be even easier. If Barrie and Bruce had tested when I started my search in 2005, I might have met my birthmother before she passed on in 2011 at the age of 95. How I would have liked to ask her a few questions.

In the case of my birth-father, all the signs point to him and I am related through DNA. However, I am reluctant to say 100% it is him. After spending six years looking at Jean McMeans and finding all the pieces of the puzzle coming together showing she was my birthmother but not finding a link through DNA, I wonder if I missed something looking at my birth father. We do show a connection through DNA, so he probably is the one.

When Barrie entered my life, it changed everything. There was DNA proof, there were people on the ground proof, in real time. Absolutely no chance this isn't the truth.

Epilogue

You might ask why I waited so long to make this search. When I was younger, I was leery of what I might find. I had no idea what kind of people my birth parents might be. I didn't want to know if they were in prison or worse. It was also very hard to trace people like that unless you hired a professional investigator. I had more important things to do at the time. I had to put this off until after my loving "adopted" parents passed. I would not have wanted to possibly hurt their feelings.

Think about all the marvelous inventions that have taken place since 1935. They all made it easier to search for anything. When computers became common in the 80's and then the internet, it became easy to search for any subject under the sun and some above it. When the Genealogy sites appeared, it became very tempting to use their services. Finally, when I received a DNA test kit for Christmas, from my wife Jane, the door was opened to me.

At first, I was just curious about the difference between my "information" sheet and my real ethnicity. Finally, at age 69, I decided to go for it and start a full-blown search for who I am. I was retired by then and had the time and inclination to do this. I remember sitting for hours at a time in front of the iMac, printing pages of facts that might be relevant. It became a game for me, testing my ability to find facts that were sometimes deeply hidden. I was my own detective, learning as I went along, always discovering new material that sometimes explained everything, like putting a giant jigsaw puzzle together, sometimes with missing pieces to be found.

This is not something with a quick solution. It took a very thorough search of every fact I could find, on a multitude of people before coming to any conclusion. When my sister Barrie showed up, I was investigating a string of 23 names associated with the Wheeler name. Evelyn was number 23. The next step would have been to search each family group and check out all the sources, life stories, census, military records and more family trees. I would have eventually discovered Evelyn was missing from a Family Tree but was right there in the census. The information was there. I just had to dig it out. I was lucky to have the "info" sheet, even if the names were fictitious. It had other clues in it that were helpful.

As time goes by and more people take advantage of DNA testing and are listed in programs like Ancestry and 23andMe, it will be much easier to trace your genealogy. In the end, DNA is the only proof of identity. It is even allowed in the Justice System because it has been proven to be accurate. Knowing the amount of centimorgans you share with a person is a big clue. The Genealogy programs will tell you their calculated opinion of the relationship. In the case of my siblings, Ancestry's opinion was first cousin or close family. If a person is a relative of one of your DNA relatives, you have to look more closely to figure out if you are blood related or just a son-in-law or something. Genealogy programs can't make an opinion on someone who hasn't tested their DNA.

If you're adopted, be prepared for people to have denial. Sometimes it's tough for them to realize a relative might have had a child that was adopted. There still is a slight stigma about the subject for some people. It's not my fault I was adopted, but some are not enlightened enough to know that. How I got here is not important enough to overlook who I am and what I am today. We don't all have the luxury of being born to married parents in a "normal" way. You are what you make of yourself, despite things that may be termed as a hardship for some. One person's hard ship might be another person's character builder. If you're handed everything you want, you may not appreciate what you have. When you earn the money and buy things, you definitely take care of them, especially when you are young and don't have much earning power. The lessons I learned, growing up, have served me well all my life. I naturally passed them on to my three daughters. They thanked me, later on in life, for teaching them how to work, and they have been praised by their employers for their work ethic. So maybe that was a good thing to pass on. Of course, they are good kids anyway.

Some of the things I have learned, in my life:

- ☆ Appreciate what you have. Some don't have anything.

- ☆ Have patience and persevere. Keep at it until you get the result you want. It may take a while, but it will be worth it.

- ☆ Take care of what you have, be it people or things. People want to know they are loved and appreciated. Tell them often.

- ☆ Things are easier. If you can't fix them, learn how, or buy a special tool, or both. If you can fix something with a new tool, when you're done you still have the tool.

- ☆ Find a way to make a living that is rewarding and satisfying to you. I feel this is more important than just making a lot of money.

- ☆ Be kind to small animals. They can sense if you mean them no harm and will respond in kind.
- ☆ Save some of your money. It may come in handy someday, for you, or someone else.
- ☆ Volunteer your services to someone or some cause. It'll help them, and make you feel good.
- ☆ Be respectful of everybody, no matter their position in life, or job title. Everyone deserves that.
- ☆ You are no better than anyone else. Some may be more privileged, but that doesn't make them any more deserving.
- ☆ Be humble in the presence of nature and respect and care for it.
- ☆ Be responsible for people who are counting on you. They deserve it.
- ☆ Be honest in all your actions. It will make you feel better about everything. If you cheat to get ahead, it won't make you feel fulfilled.
- ☆ Be punctual. Get to work early. Meet people when you say you will. I think it's a sign of respect.
- ☆ Do everything as well as you are able. No one can complain if you're doing the best, you can.
- ☆ Never quit learning. There is always something new to learn, or something old to perfect.

☆ *Thank You* ☆

Family Trees

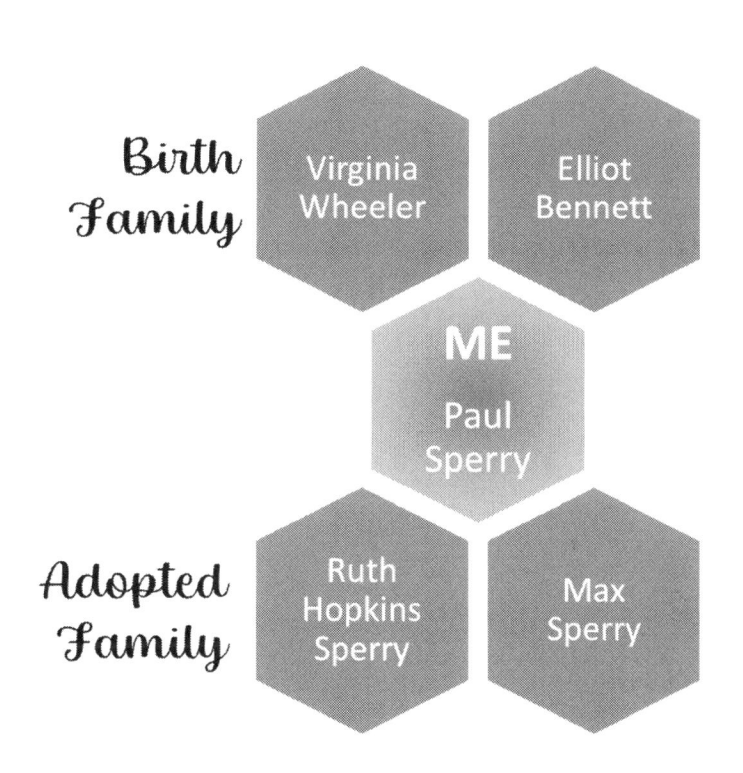

Birth Family
- Virginia Wheeler
- Elliot Bennett

ME
Paul Sperry

Adopted Family
- Ruth Hopkins Sperry
- Max Sperry

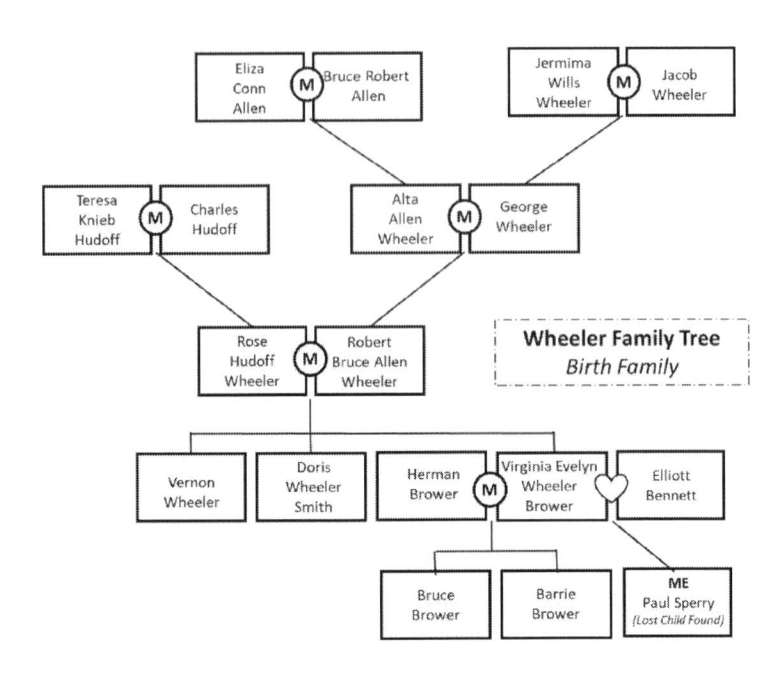

Lost Child Found

Wheeler Family Tree
Birth Family

- Eliza Conn Allen (M) Bruce Robert Allen
- Jermima Wills Wheeler (M) Jacob Wheeler
- Teresa Knieb Hudoff (M) Charles Hudoff
- Alta Allen Wheeler (M) George Wheeler
- Rose Hudoff Wheeler (M) Robert Bruce Allen Wheeler
  - Vernon Wheeler
  - Doris Wheeler Smith
  - Herman Brower (M) Virginia Evelyn Wheeler Brower ♡ Elliott Bennett
    - Bruce Brower
    - Barrie Brower
    - **ME** Paul Sperry *(Lost Child Found)*

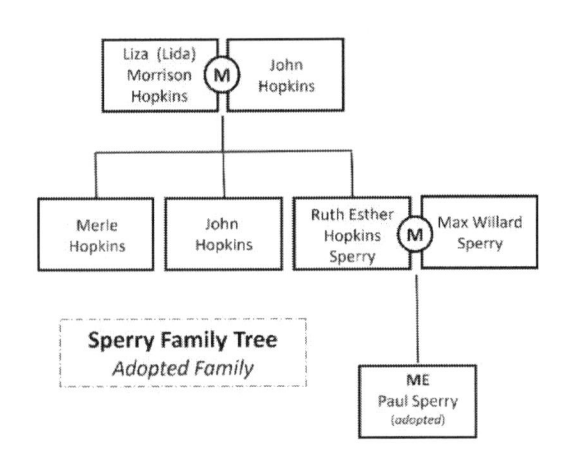

Sperry Family Tree
Adopted Family

- Liza (Lida) Morrison Hopkins (M) John Hopkins
  - Merle Hopkins
  - John Hopkins
  - Ruth Esther Hopkins Sperry (M) Max Willard Sperry
    - **ME** Paul Sperry *(adopted)*

Questions to Ponder
for you or your Book Club

1. What was your favorite part of the book?
2. Which story or part of the book stuck with you?
3. If you were adopted, would you want to find your birth family?
4. Did you reread any passages? Which ones?
5. What surprised you most about the book?
6. How would finding your birth family change the relationship with your adopted family?
7. Did your opinion of the book change as you read it?
8. If you could ask the author anything, what would it be?
9. How did the book impact you? Will you reflect back on it in a few months or years?
10. Who do you want to share this book with?
11. Are there lingering questions from the book you're still thinking about?
12. In the Epilogue, which of the lessons learned was the most meaningful to you? Why?

Lost Child Found

Acronym Decoder

O   O gauge trains, scale 1:43 to 1:48
16mm 16-millimeter movie film
24/7 24-hours-a-day / 7-days-a-week

AM-FM Early radio (amplitude & frequency modulation)
AFB   Air Force Base

B-25   North American B-25 Mitchell Aircraft
B-36   Convair B-36 Peacemaker Aircraft
B-52   Boeing B-52 Stratofortress Aircraft
B.C.   British Columbia, Canada
BSA   BSA Motorcycle Company

c.   circa (approximately)
CB   Citizens Band Radio
CCC   Civilian Conservation Corps
CHP   California Highway Patrol
C.S.D. Constant Speed Drive
CQ   Night CQ (Charge of Quarters) runners

dba   doing business as
DNA   Deoxyribonucleic acid, hereditary material

EPR   Engine Pressure Ratio

F-102 Convair F-102 Delta Dagger Aircraft
FBI   Federal Bureau of Investigation
FM   Frequency Modulation

G.I.   General Issue (low rank military personnel)
GM   General Motors

Lost Child Found

HO	HO gauge trains, scale 1:87
HiFi	High Fidelity Stereo System
hp	Horse Power
HTD	Heavy Truck Driver

J-57   Pratt & Whitney J-57 Aircraft Engine

KC-135 Boeing KC-135 Stratotanker Aircraft
KC-97 Boeing KC-97 Stratofreighter Aircraft

L.A.   Los Angeles

mpg   Miles Per Gallon
mph   Miles Per Hour

OMG   Oh My God

PCD   Pipeline Construction Division of East Bay Water
P.I.E.   Pacific Intermountain Express
psi   Pounds per Square Inch

RN   Registered Nurse
RPM   Revolutions Per Minute

SAC   Strategic Air command

T.I.   Training Instructor
ttyl   Talk To You Later
TV   Television

U-2   Lockheed U-2 Spy Plane
U.C.   University of California

V-8 Eight-cylinder piston engine in a V configuration
VW   Volkswagen

WPA Works Progress Administration
WW2 World War II

Made in the USA
Monee, IL
30 October 2023